IESE CITIES IN MOTION:
INTERNATIONAL URBAN BEST PRACTICES

CITIES AND
THE ENVIRONMENT
THE CHALLENGE OF
BECOMING GREEN AND SUSTAINABLE

VOLUME 1

PROF. PASCUAL BERRONE
PROF. JOAN ENRIC RICART COSTA
ANA ISABEL DUCH T-FIGUERAS

Preface to the Book Series

"IESE CITIES IN MOTION:
International urban best practices"

The world is experiencing the largest increase in the urbanization rate in history. Today, more than half of the world's population lives in cities and it is forecast that the percentage of urban residents in the global population will increase to almost 70% by 2050. This unprecedented growth in urbanization has the potential to bring significant benefits for citizens, such as new jobs and well-being, along with overall economic growth. However, rapid urbanization also multiplies the number, size and complexity of the challenges faced by cities, such as increasing pressure on scarce resources, greater demand for basic infrastructure and public services, as well as greater socioeconomic inequality.

Cities must be able to solve economic, social and environmental problems simultaneously, in all cases with the aim of improving the welfare and quality of life of their residents. In their search for sustainable, equitable, connected and innovative city models, municipal leaders around the world look at the experiences of other cities to get ideas and study best practices. Although there is no "one size fits all" solution, this book series aims to help city managers in their endeavors to create urban areas that are environmentally, economically and socially sustainable. With this objective, this series will examine some of the actions, projects and initiatives that have had the best results in cities internationally, so that other cities around the world can build on the most successful approaches and adapt them to their local realities and needs.

The book series is structured on the basis of the IESE Cities in Motion model, which includes an innovative approach to the governance of cities and a new urban model for the 21st century based on 10 key areas or dimensions: human capital, social cohesion, the economy, public management, governance, mobility and transportation, the environment, urban planning, technology, and international outreach. Each volume in this series provides an overview of the main challenges regarding a specific dimension and exhibits some of the most successful initiatives and actions that have been adopted in regard to that area in different cities around the world. Despite the fact that each area is covered in a separate volume of its own, all the key areas must be seen as different parts of a system that works as one. All the dimensions are interconnected and actions in one area affect other areas at the same time. Therefore, the available resources must be shared and managed together in order to achieve sustainable, lively, healthy and safe cities.

With this book series we aim to contribute to the debate on smart urban governance by developing valuable ideas and innovative tools that can lead to smarter and more sustainable cities, while promoting real change at the local level and improving people's quality of life. We believe that current urban challenges are not only problems to be solved but also opportunities to be exploited and turned into more positive challenges.

Contents

1. Introduction

Environmental issues are deeply intertwined with urbanization processes. As centers of economic activity, cities are responsible for the vast majority of the world's energy use and global greenhouse gas (GHG) emissions. In fact, **even though urban centers cover less than 2% of the Earth's surface, they are responsible for some 60% to 80% of global energy consumption and around 70% of GHG emissions**[1] (New Climate Economy, 2014; Seto et al., 2014; UN-Habitat, 2012a). Cities are therefore major contributors to global climate change.

The decades to come are expected to experience significant urban population growth, which will lead to the expansion of urban infrastructure. This development will increase the emissions from the transport, buildings and industry sectors, along with a rise in global energy demand. In a business-as-usual scenario, by 2050 the expansion of urban infrastructure alone is projected to generate 470 gigatons (Gt) of CO_2 (IPCC, 2014), which is equivalent in weight to 68.15 billion African elephants or more than 2.82 billion blue whales.[2,3] These trends will intensify the brutality of some of the greatest challenges of the 21st century: climate change,

---

[1] The sources consulted give different percentages of carbon dioxide (CO_2) emissions and global energy use by cities. For instance, according to Seto et al. (2014), "urban areas account for between 71% and 76% of CO_2 emissions from global final energy use and between 67% and 76% of global energy use." Other sources, such as UN-Habitat, estimate that cities are responsible for 78% of the world's energy use and more than 60% of all carbon dioxide produced (UN-Habitat, 2012a).

[2] A single gigaton (Gt) is 1 billion (1,000,000,000) metric tons. A male African elephant weighs some 6.8 metric tons, so a gigaton is the equivalent of more than 147 million African elephants. Similarly, a blue whale can weigh up to 146 metric tons, so a gigaton is the weight of more than six million blue whales (source: Mooney, 2015).

[3] Gigatons of carbon dioxide ($GtCO_2$) is not the same as gigatons of carbon emissions (GtC). It is important to bear this difference in mind, since the values vary extensively from one to the other.

global warming and energy security, as well as many other environmental problems in terms of pollution of air, water and land.

However, despite being major contributors to these challenges, cities can be at the same time part of the solution. **Although environmental issues are mostly global**, **city administrations can also be very influential**. The way that cities grow and operate has a direct impact on their energy demand and, as a result, on GHG emissions and climate change. Improving environmental sustainability through urban strategies and plans to fight pollution, supporting green buildings and alternative sources of energy, as well as the efficient management of water and waste can significantly reverse the current trends.

In addition to these tendencies, we also find a change in people's preferences and behavior. City dwellers are becoming more and more concerned about their impact on the planet and they are increasingly demanding cleaner, healthier and higher-quality urban places to live in. According to a recent study by the Pew Research Center, climate change is seen as a top global threat in 19 of the 40 nations surveyed (Carle, 2015). Additionally, at a city level, in a survey carried out by the London School of Economics and Political Science, ICLEI and the Global Green Growth Institute in 90 cities covering all the populated continents, 70% of the survey respondents identified air pollution as a significant or very significant environmental challenge for their city. This was followed by severe storms and flooding (68%), storm water management (64%), and solid waste processing and disposal (57%), as well as household waste, water pollution and lack of green space (Rode and Floater, 2013). Therefore, environmental challenges are becoming an important and increasing concern for urban populations.

Yet environmental issues are not always a priority for city-level leadership. **Sustainability is a long-term issue, requiring investment for**

long-term benefit. Policy makers in city councils around the world face crucial choices in order to transform the challenges posed by global climate change into opportunities, while solving residents' short-term basic needs. However, policy makers need to understand that climate change has the risk of affecting urban areas not only ecologically but also economically, socially and culturally. As a result, it is in the residents' best interest to invest in sustainable urban development.

City administrations need to create strong and smart urban policies to develop sustainable urban energy systems that can simultaneously improve people's quality of life and their environment. Local governments are well positioned to tackle the new environmental and energy challenges, since cities are connected to a larger world (regional, national and global). **The type of cities that will be developed and the type of policies that will be implemented within urban areas in the years to come will be critical for the future of energy systems, climate change and the environment.**

***

Section 2, the next part of this volume, sets out the historical, current and future trends and impacts of urbanization on the environment. Section 3 assesses different solutions and strategies for sustainable urban development, as well as highlighting some international urban best practices. The book concludes with a list of learning points with respect to the environment and the mitigation of climate change in urban areas.

***

2. Environmental Trends and Challenges in Cities

Urbanization and climate change are coevolving in dangerous ways, threatening to have very negative economic, social and environmental impacts, aside from a direct effect on people's quality of life and well-being. Adapting to climate change can therefore reduce risks and benefit people, economies and ecosystems.

Climate change and global warming refer to an increase in average global temperatures, mainly due to human activities and natural events. The Earth's surface temperature has increased by 0.74 °C to 1.8 °C since 1906 and, based on current trends, it is expected to increase by up to 4 °C during the 21st century unless action is taken (UN-Habitat, 2008a). If this happens and climate change and global warming are not stopped, extreme weather, periods of severe heat and cold, storms, droughts, flooding, rising sea levels and soil erosion will be inevitable, affecting our planet in various ways.

Figure 1: Large cities and climate-related hazards (cyclones, flooding, landslides and droughts)

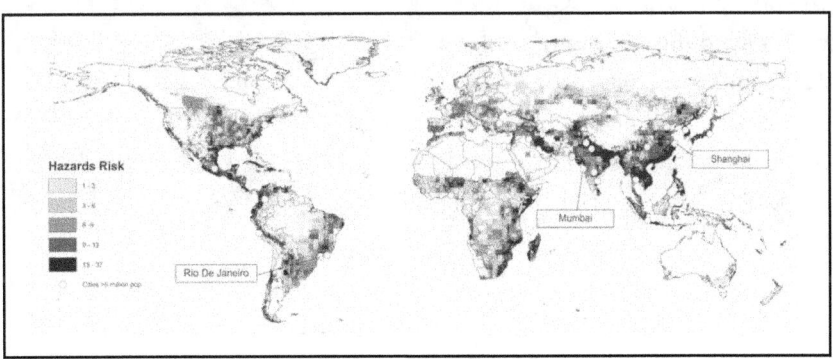

Source: De Sherbinin, Schiller and Pulsipher, 2007.

Most human and economic activities are concentrated in urban areas, making cities major contributors to global climate change. The impact of cities on global warming and climate change basically derives from the production and consumption of energy (see point 2.2), as well as other resources such as water (see point 2.3) and other material resources. In addition, cities and towns are not only major contributors to global warming but are also particularly vulnerable to climate change. Developing urban areas and cities in coastal zones are affected to a greater extent. In fact, many major coastal cities with populations of more than 10 million people are already under threat, with cities in Southeast Asia more vulnerable to flooding (Floater and Rode, 2014; UN-Habitat, 2012a).

GHG emissions

This increase in average global temperatures is caused primarily by rises in GHG emissions, such as carbon dioxide (CO_2), methane (CH_4), nitrous oxide (N_2O) and sulfur hexafluoride (SF_6). **The main gas responsible for global warming and climate change is CO_2, which accounts for some 75% of all GHG emissions.** In 2013, global CO_2 emissions alone reached almost 36 gigatons of CO_2 ($GtCO_2$), which, using the

Table 1: GHG emissions in selected cities

City	GHG emissions (tons of CO_2 eq. per capita)	Year
Bangkok	10.70	2005
Beijing	10.10	2006
Cape Town	11.60	2005
Frankfurt	13.70	2005
Mexico City	4.25	2007
Prague	9.40	2005
São Paulo	1.40	2000
Seoul	4.10	2006
Sydney	0.88	2006
Tokyo	4.89	2006
Vancouver	4.90	2006
Washington	19.70	2005

Source: Based on Mutizwa-Mangiza et al., 2011.

same comparison as in the introduction, is equivalent to 5.22 billion African elephants or more than 216 million blue whales (Olivier et al., 2014).

Traditionally, developed cities have contributed more to global emissions than developing countries, but now cities in emerging economies are reaching the levels of developed cities. (See Table 1 and Figure 2.)

Figure 2: Carbon emissions in selected countries and cities

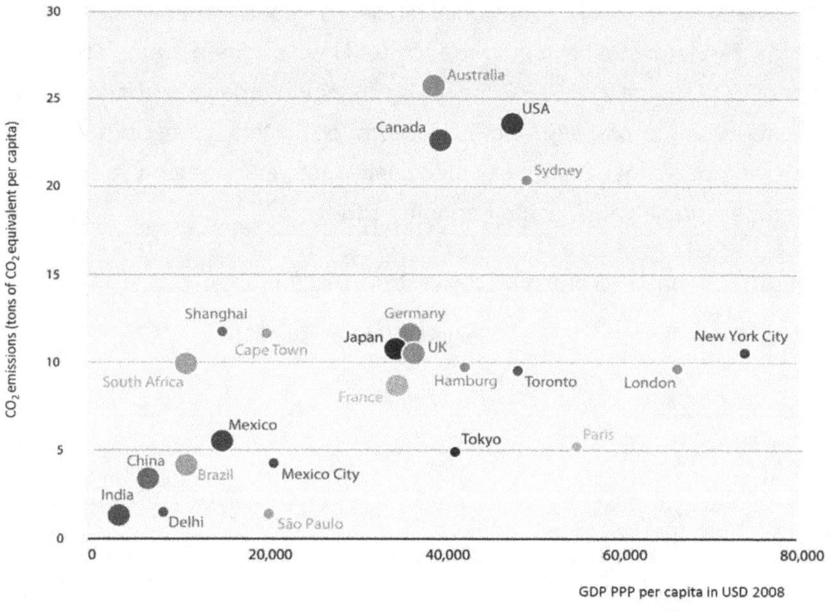

GDP PPP per capita in USD 2008

Source: Rode and Burdett, 2011.

The burning and consumption of fossil fuels (oil, gas and coal) **are among the main contributors to global climate change, being responsible for some 60% of greenhouse gas emissions** (UN-Habitat, 2008a). By fuel, coal and oil are the most responsible for global CO_2 emissions, with 43.9% and 35.3% respectively in 2012 (IEA, 2014c). By sector, energy accounts for the largest share of global GHG emissions, with electricity, heating, transport and industry combined generating more than 60% of global GHG (UNHabitat, 2008a).

Despite all these challenges, climate change can also be a source of opportunities to readdress patterns of production and consumption of cities and individuals. **Urban areas are centers of innovation that can develop strategies to deal with climate change**, creating opportunities to reduce or mitigate GHG emissions and enhancing sustainability and resilience (Mutizwa-Mangiza et al., 2011). For instance, some analysts estimate that the world's 724 largest cities could reduce GHG emissions by up to 1.5 billion tons of CO_2 annually by 2030, mainly by changing urban transport systems (see the volume *Mobility and Transportation* in this series) but also by improving buildings' energy efficiency and waste management, along with other measures (New Climate Economy, 2014).

Figure 3: Global GHG emissions by sector, 2012 ($MtCO_2e$)

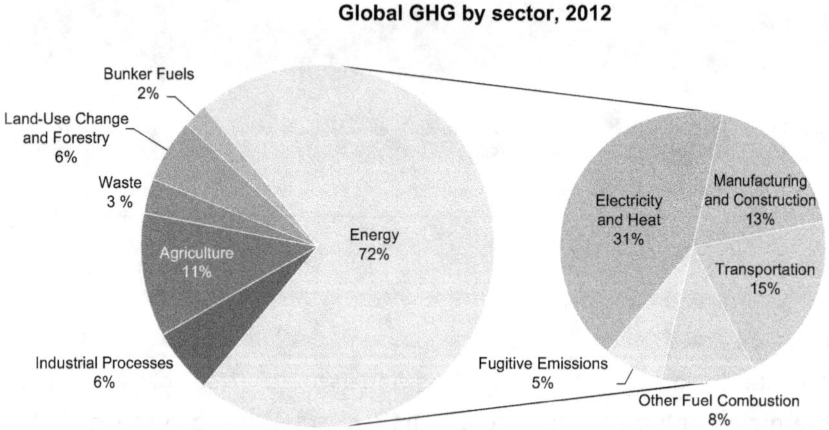

Global GHG by sector, 2012

Bunker Fuels
2%

Land-Use Change
and Forestry
6%

Waste
3 %

Agriculture
11%

Industrial Processes
6%

Energy
72%

Electricity
and Heat
31%

Manufacturing
and Construction
13%

Transportation
15%

Fugitive Emissions
5%

Other Fuel Combustion
8%

Source: Prepared by the authors based on CAIT Climate Data Explorer, World Resources Institute.

***

2.1 Air Quality and Noise Pollution

Air pollution

Bad-quality air puts people at additional risk of serious, long-term health problems. In 2006 the World Health Organization (WHO) estimated that 24% of the global disease burden and 23% of all deaths could be attributed to environmental factors (Prüss-Üstün and Corvalán, 2006). According to the OECD, **air pollution is projected to become the world's top environmental cause of premature mortality by 2050** (OECD, 2012). Moreover, the WHO estimated that in 2012 alone air pollution was linked to some seven million premature deaths, with a total of 3.3 million deaths linked to indoor air pollution and 2.6 million deaths related to outdoor air pollution (WHO, 2014a).

Figure 4: PM$_{10}$ levels for selected cities by region, 2008–2012

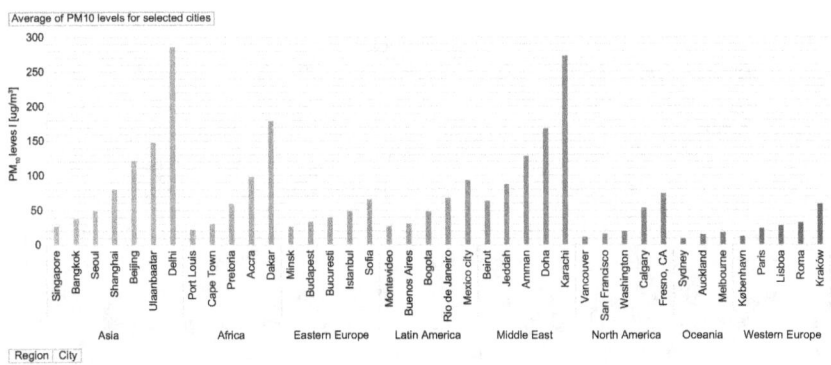

Source: Prepared by the authors based on WHO Ambient Air Pollution Database, 2014.

Man-made air pollution, which results largely from combustion processes, contains many toxic components. One of the most important in urban areas is particulate matter (PM), exposure to which has been associated with many different effects on health. Urban air pollution accounts for the largest proportion of global air pollution, as a result of rapid urbanization rates in major cities, especially in developing countries. In general, PM_{10} and $PM_{2.5}$, which is the smallest and most dangerous type of particulate matter, are the most common indicators of exposure to urban air pollution.

According to the WHO's urban air quality database,[4] only 12% of people living in cities report an air quality that complies with the WHO air quality guideline levels (WHO, 2014b). Moreover, about half of the urban population being monitored is exposed to a level of air pollution that is at least 2.5 times higher than the levels the WHO recommends. More precisely, in the 15 countries with the highest GHG emissions, "the damage to health from poor air quality is valued at an average of about 4% of national GDP" (Fang, 2014).

BOX 1: New Delhi has the worst quality air in the world, while Beijing is improving

According to the WHO's ambient air pollution database 2014, New Delhi has been reported as being the city with the world's most toxic air, with an annual average of 153 micrograms of $PM_{2.5}$ per cubic meter. This is six times higher than the maximum the WHO recommends. New Delhi is so polluted that some experts suggest that inhaling the city's air is equivalent to smoking between 10 and 20 cigarettes a day (Burke, 2015; Thiagarajan, 2015).

In the Indian capital, private vehicles are responsible for some 40% to 50% of the dangerous $PM_{2.5}$ particulates (Burke, 2015). And this situation does not seem to be getting any better, as 1,400 more cars are added to the Indian capital's streets every day (CNN, 2015). Other sources of pollution and smog are the poor quality of fuel and the high levels of biomass burned in winter.

On current trends, this bad air quality has been estimated to cut up to three years off the lives of millions of Indians living in New Delhi's metropolitan area (CNN, April 14, 2015). The WHO also found that India has the world's highest rate of death from respiratory disease, with 159 per 100,000 in 2012, about 10 times

---

[4] The WHO air quality database 2014 consists of annual means for PM_{10} and $PM_{2.5}$ and covers almost 1,600 cities across 91 countries from 2008 to 2013.

that of Italy, five times that of the United Kingdom and twice that of China (Burke, 2015).

Air pollution in New Delhi – Lotus Temple

Photo: Ana Isabel Duch.

In fact, New Delhi's pollution levels are now 45% to 50% higher than those in Beijing. The Chinese capital, despite still being one of the most polluted cities in the world, has improved its pollution levels since 2012. This is the result of different actions taken by the authorities, such as restricting vehicles on the roads and restricting the production of some highly polluting factories.

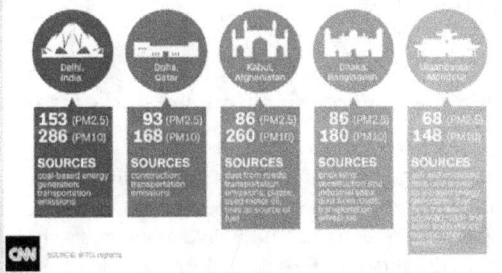

Although economic development is the top priority for India, this is a serious concern and the governments of New Delhi and of other cities in India will have to initiate some programs to solve the pollution problem, increasing energy efficiency and reducing emissions. Otherwise, the problem will only worsen.

Noise pollution

Another often underestimated environmental health problem in cities is **noise pollution.** Urban noise not only affects people's quality of life but can also cause serious and long-term harm to health. According to a report by the WHO, environmental noise can have specific health effects on people, including cardiovascular diseases, cognitive impairment, sleep disturbance, stress and hearing problems (WHO, 2011).

Cities have many sources of noise. The most significant is probably related to road traffic but other sources are industrial noises, such as building construction and mechanical ventilation systems.

As seen in this point, air and noise pollution not only have negative consequences for people's health and quality of life, they also negatively affect cities' economic growth and attractiveness to talent (New Climate Economy, 2014). For all these reasons, city administrations around the world are increasingly concerned about improving air quality and reducing noise pollution in their cities. (See Box 2.)

BOX 2: Measuring and mapping air quality and noise pollution

Many researchers in cities around the world are creating new equipment to crowdsource environmental data, showing an increasing concern about air quality and noise pollution in cities. New digital technologies help measure and map air and noise pollution by offering accurate data much more cheaply than professional equipment (Saunders and Baeck, 2015). The data are collected through sensors and digital sensing equipment that measure air and noise pollution and allow policy makers to decide about air quality and noise levels in their cities.

Air quality

Some good examples of this technology are the London Air API or application programming interface (http://www.londonair.org.uk/LondonAir/API), produced by a group of researchers of King's College London, which measures and maps air pollution with digital sensing equipment, and the PiMi Airbox by Tsinghua University (http://www.pimiair.com/data), which measures indoor air pollution in Beijing, China.

Noise pollution

Another good example of mapping noise in cities is the NoiseTube app, which uses the GPS and microphones of smartphones to record and gather data and create collaborative noise maps, which can be far more detailed than the official versions. The project started in 2008 and aims to help communities that want to tackle noise pollution collaboratively, taking control and monitoring their own noise levels (Rust, 2014). As of 2014, the app has been used in communities in various European cities, such as Brussels and Antwerp, and has been downloaded by 10,000 people, with 2,700 people registered on the NoiseTube website (Rust, 2014).

These initiatives can be very useful both for city administrators, who can get a crowdsourced map of the air pollution in their cities to use when making decisions, and city dwellers, who can have information about the air quality in their homes and about the noise pollution in their neighborhoods.

***

2.2 Energy Consumption

Energy is needed for the vast majority of cities' activities: transport, industrial and commercial activities, buildings and infrastructure, water distribution, food production, etc. Therefore, energy is vital to modern urban economies. However, our current energy systems have many market failures, in particular those related to the environmental impact of pollution from fossil fuel extraction and combustion.

Energy use has grown by more than 50% since 1990 and global energy demand is expected to grow by between 20% and 35% in the next 15 years (New Climate Economy, 2014). Global demand for electricity alone is expected to grow by 56% between 2010 and 2040 (Hower, 2015). Most of this increase will come from developing countries.

Urban areas account for the vast bulk of this demand. **Cities consume today about 75% of the global primary energy used**. Moreover, **if current trends in urban expansion continue, they are expected to consume three times more energy in 2050 compared with 2005** (Creutzig et al., 2014).

Different sectors contribute to energy consumption: industry, the building sector and the transport sector account for the majority of this consumption, while agriculture, land use change, waste and commercial and public services account for the rest. (See Figure 5.)

Figure 5: Total global energy demand by sector, 2012

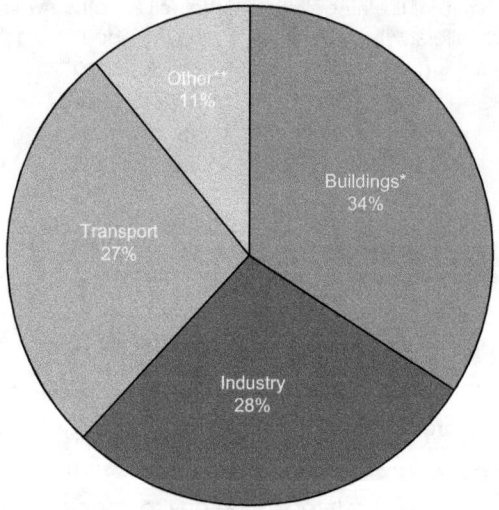

Other**
11%

Buildings*
34%

Transport
27%

Industry
28%

Source: Prepared by the authors based on IEA, 2012 (as cited in IPEEC©2007–2016)

Note: *Buildings (residential and commercial);
     **Other (including agriculture and non-energy use).

The building sector

Buildings consume vast amounts of energy at all stages of their lives (raw materials, the construction process, maintenance, lighting, air conditioning, cleaning, etc.). In fact, **the building sector is one of the major contributors to the strain on the environment, responsible for some 30% to 35% of global energy consumption and more than 20% of GHG emissions** (Sustainable Urban Futures, 2015; UN-Habitat, 2008b).

In the developed world some 40% of energy end use takes place in buildings, while in the developing world the figure is still 20% (Floater and Rode, 2014). However, as much of the future growth in urbanization will take place in cities in developing Asia and Africa, this percentage will increase. In China, for example, 60% of all buildings will be new buildings by 2020 (Schwarz, 2010).

Hong Kong skyline at night.

Source: Pixabay, CC0.

Energy and income

As income rises, so does energy supply: high-income countries consume more than 14 times as much energy per capita as the least developed countries, and seven times as much as lower-middle-income countries (New Climate Economy, 2014). (See Figure 6.)

Figure 6: Energy use vs. GDP per capita in selected cities

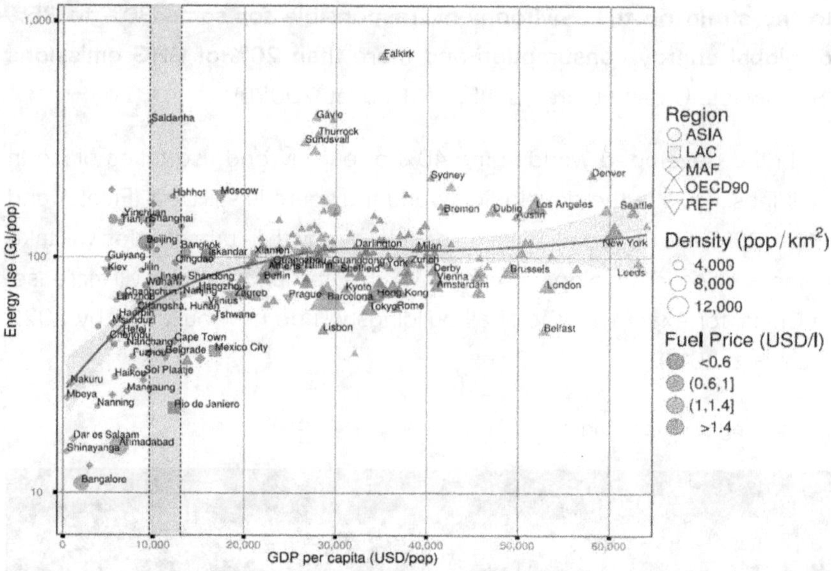

Source: Creutzig et al., 2014.

Moreover, as previously mentioned, in the industrialized world the building sector represents a higher proportion of energy consumption while, in developing and emerging cities, the transport and industry sectors account for a higher percentage of total energy consumption. (See Figure 7.)

Figure 7: Energy consumption in selected cities

Energy consumption in selected cities in high-income countries (%)

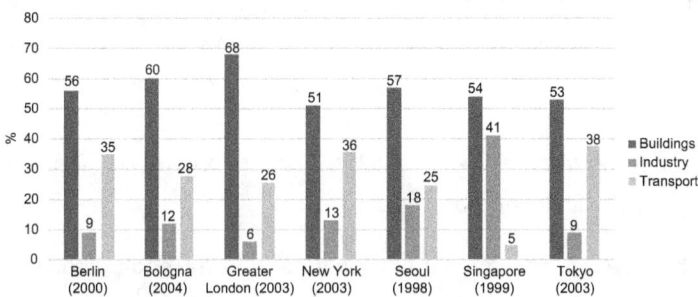

Energy consumption in selected cities in middle-income countries (%)

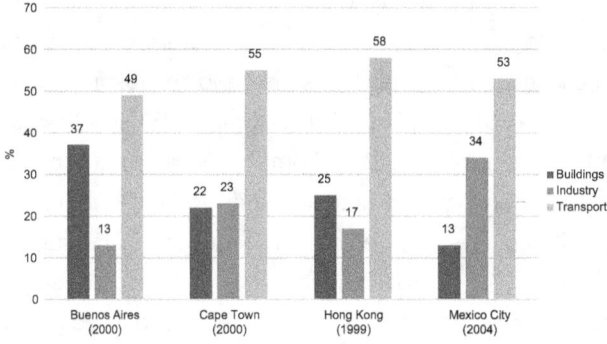

Energy consumption in selected Asian cities (%)

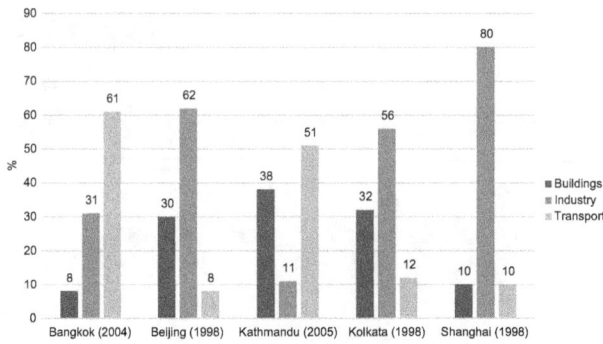

Source: Prepared by the authors based on UN-Habitat Global Urban Observatory 2008, in UN-Habitat, 2008b.

Fossil fuels still account for most of the world's energy supply. In 2012, the world's total primary energy supply consisted of 81.7% fossil fuels (oil, coal and gas), 4.8% nuclear power and only 13.5% renewable energy sources (such as hydro, biofuels and waste, wind, geothermic and solar) (IEA, 2014c). This expansion of fossil fuels is accountable for most of the current energy challenges. In order to have a sustainable future and stop climate change, we need to reverse the current trends and fulfill the world's energy needs with low-carbon sources.

Carbon-based energy generation has a large ecological footprint, which is a good measure of sustainability (UN-Habitat, 2012b). The "ecological footprint" could be defined as "the impact of an individual, a city, a country, or the whole global population measured in terms of the area of biologically productive land and water required to produce the resources and goods they consume and to absorb the waste they generate" (UN-Habitat, 2008b; WWF Global, 2015). In other words, how much countries or individuals take from the environment to produce and consume goods vs. what they actually have. Today, humanity's ecological footprint is 2.2 hectares (ha) per person, more than 21% greater than the Earth's biocapacity (1.8 ha) (UN-Habitat, 2008b). Proportionally, developed countries are responsible for much more of the world's ecological footprint.

Figure 8: Ecological footprint of selected cities

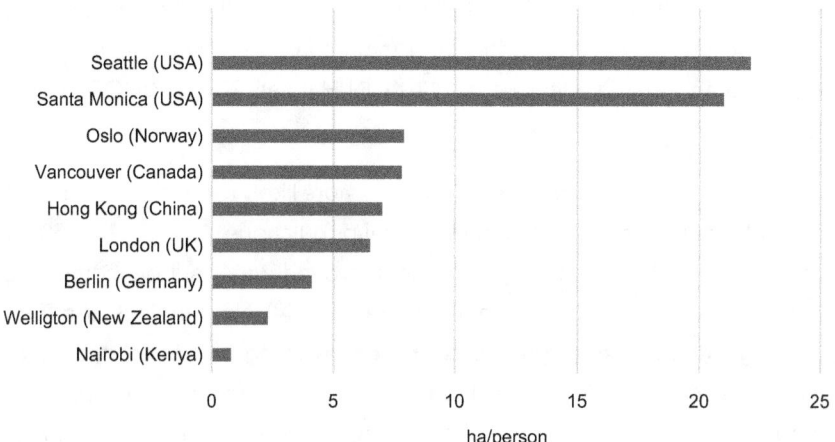

Source: Prepared by the authors based on UN-Habitat Global Urban Observatory 2008, in UN-Habitat, 2008b.

However, at the same time, cities play an important role in the solution. More and more cities are becoming hubs of innovation in alternative and renewable energy sources, reducing their dependence on fossil fuels and implementing strategies to improve the current urban energy situation and reduce climate change. Some of these solutions and strategies will be analyzed in Section 3.

***

2.3 Water and Sanitation

One of the main challenges affecting the sustainability of human urban settlements is the lack of access to safe water and sanitation. A clean and healthy city should guarantee its residents access to clean and safe water for drinking and other uses. However, although huge improvements have been made in the past decades in this field – we moved from four million individuals having access to improved drinking water in 1990 to six million people in 2010 – around 700 million to one billion individuals still lack access to clean and safe water, and more than 2.6 billion do not have access to adequate sanitation facilities (UN-Habitat, 2012c; WHO/UNICEF, 2014).

Urban populations are, in general terms, more likely to have better access to a water supply and sanitation than rural populations. As of 2012, 96% of the urban population globally used an improved water supply compared with 82% of the rural population (World Bank, 2014). Nonetheless, **the fast-growing rates of city populations are jeopardizing improved access to safe water**, since the increase in the use of drinking water resources is not keeping up with the urban population growth. Likewise, major progress in the use of improved sanitation is also undermined by population growth. (See Figure 9.)

Figure 9: Urban population with access to improved drinking water and sanitation

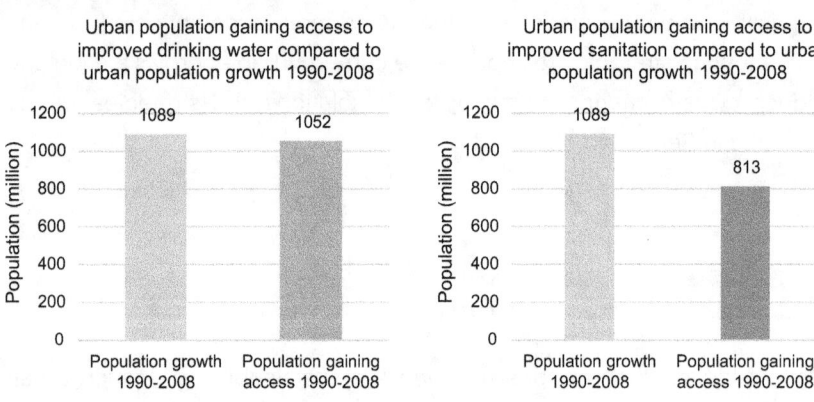

Source: Prepared by the authors based on WHO/UNICEF, 2010.

There are still huge intra-urban inequalities. In particular, those who suffer the most are the individuals living in slums or informal settlements in developing cities. They tend to have lower access to an improved water supply and insufficient access to sanitation services, since they need to share insufficient and poorly managed resources and systems (Floater and Rode, 2014; WHO/UNICEF, 2014). Paradoxically, in many cases low-income urban inhabitants have to pay high prices for water, sometimes up to 50 times the price paid by higher-income city dwellers (UN-Habitat, 2012c). As a result, improving water supply in informal settlements in developing cities may require innovative approaches, such as pay-as-you-go services offered at water kiosks or public water points (WHO/UNICEF, 2014). For instance, according to a report produced jointly by the WHO and UNICEF, people living in informal settlements in Mombasa, Kenya, rely much more on water kiosks and have less access to piped supplies on premises compared with the average levels of coverage in the rest of urban Kenya (WHO/UNICEF, 2014).

These problems have vast consequences for human health, well-being and safety. For instance, the absence of proper sanitation facilities increases the contamination of water resources, which poses important health risks to the urban poor. Moreover, water management systems also affect the environment and economic growth. Since water is typically heated using natural gas or electricity, water management and water distribution are huge energy consumers.

Consequently, enhancing coverage and access to drinking water in cities as well as improving water management systems are important challenges to be tackled – and are crucial during urban development. **Cities cannot be sustainable without ensuring reliable access to safe drinking water and adequate sanitation**.

***

2.4 Waste and Disposal

Waste is a direct outcome of human activities. As income per capita rises, the volume of items we produce and consume also increases. As a consequence, the amount of waste we are generating is reaching worrisome levels. According to some estimates, **in a business-as-usual scenario, global solid waste rates will triple by 2100, exceeding 11 million tons per day** (Hoornweg et al., 2013). These levels of waste generation will have serious effects on cities and countries around the world, with social, economic and environmental costs.

Solid waste is mostly an urban phenomenon. **As urbanization increases, global solid-waste generation is speeding up**. This is of critical importance if one notes that waste generation rates are growing even more quickly than urbanization rates. In 1990, the Earth had 220 million urban inhabitants, who created less than 300,000 tons of trash per day. By 2000, the number of people living in cities had reached 2.9 billion, and they generated more than three million tons of waste per day (Hoornweg et al., 2013). And, according to a report by the World Bank, it is likely that by 2025 there will be 4.3 billion urban residents, who will generate about 2.2 billion tons of waste per year, compared with 1.3 billion tons per year in 2012 (Hoornweg and Bhada-Tata, 2012).

Effective management of municipal solid waste (MSW) **is therefore a crucial challenge for city authorities around the world.** It is one of the primary and most important services a city provides for its residents and one of the greatest costs to municipal budgets. The annual cost of the management of solid waste was projected to increase from $205 billion in 2010 to $375 billion in 2025 (World Bank, 2012).

Figure 10: Generation of municipal solid waste per capita (kg/yr) in selected cities

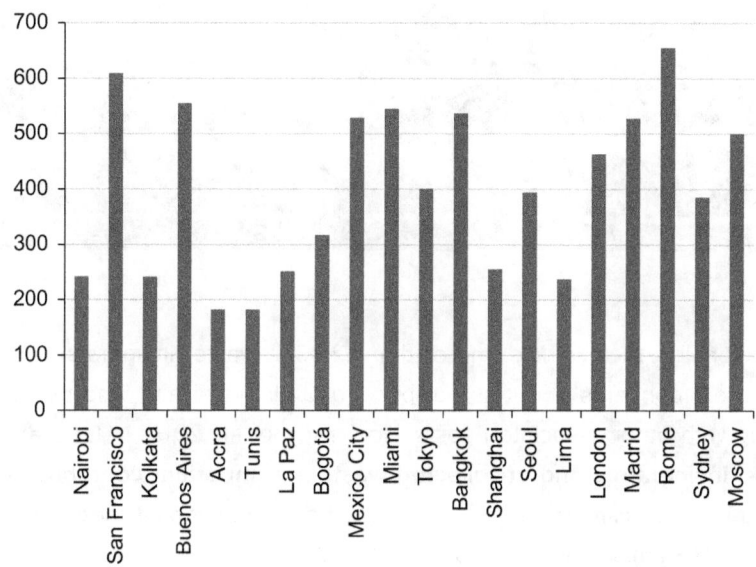

Source: Waste Atlas – D-Waste.

The waste management problem is especially critical in emerging and developing cities, which recently have faced an excessive and increasing generation of MSW (Abarca et al., 2013). These cities have scarce financial resources and a limited capacity to manage environmental issues. High amounts of MSW thus pose a significant burden on these cities' municipal budgets, and their landfills do not have enough space. For instance, the landfills of Mexico City's Bordo Poniente and Shanghai's Laogang receive more than 10,000 tons of waste per day (World Bank, 2013).

Municipal solid waste in the Indian cities of Jaipur and Varanasi

Photos: Ana Isabel Duch.

Additionally, the world's more than 2,000 waste incinerators raise important concerns about ash disposal and air, water and land pollution, along with other associated costs (Hoornweg et al., 2013). In fact, **landfill sites, incinerators and uncollected waste are important contributors to pollution and climate change through the production of methane and other GHG emissions** (World Bank, 2013). Waste management is estimated to account for 5% of the emissions of global GHG gases (1,460 $mtCO_2e$ or million tons of carbon dioxide equivalent) and 12% of total global methane emissions, mainly from landfill sites (Fang, 2014; Hoornweg and Bhada-Tata, 2012; Hoornweg et al., 2013).

Although waste management is not the biggest contributor to GHG emissions, waste management should be an important concern for governments in cities and countries around the world, taking into account the aforementioned rates of waste generation that are projected for the following decades. In fact, proper management of waste can reduce and minimize methane emissions and bring important benefits for people living in cities. In a study by the World Bank and the Climate Works Foundation it was estimated that, through integrated solid waste management in Brazil, CO_2 emissions could be reduced by between 158 million tons (megatons or Mt) and 315 Mt, valued at $4.8 billion to $9.7 billion based on the social cost of carbon. It was estimated that this would prevent at least 2,500 premature deaths from air pollution, while generating between 44,000 and 110,000 jobs, cutting Brazil's energy demand by between 0.5% and 1.1% and increasing Brazil's GDP by at least $13.3 billion between 2012 and 2032 (World Bank and ClimateWorks Foundation, 2014).

Section 3 will analyze some international best practices and initiatives to manage municipal solid waste, changing patterns of consumption and waste generation and reducing GHG emissions. **With less dense, more resource-efficient and better-managed cities, consuming fewer resources and putting in place the right initiatives, the aforementioned trends and challenges could be reversed.**

BOX 3: E-waste in Accra, Ghana

According to the United Nations University, the amount of global e-waste – that is, discarded electrical and electronic equipment – reached 41.8 million tons in 2014 (Baldé, 2015). This is equivalent to around seven times the weight of the Great Pyramid of Giza. This electronic waste is the fault mainly of developed countries, particularly the United States and European countries, with emerging countries such as China contributing more and more every year. According to the previously mentioned report, just two countries, the United States and China, discarded nearly one-third of the world's total e-waste in 2014 (Baldé, 2015). The vast majority of this e-waste goes to developing countries, mainly in Africa and Asia. Although it is illegal to import e-waste that does not comply with the Basel Convention, a lot of e-waste from developed countries goes to developing countries through unofficial channels.

The city of Accra, Ghana's capital and largest city, is one of the sites that receives most of the discarded e-waste from developed countries. Agbogbloshie, a suburb of Accra, is one of the largest e-waste dump sites in Africa. In 2013 Agbogbloshie was ranked the most toxic site on Earth. Many young people work in Agbogbloshie dismantling electronic devices without the proper safeguards against the toxic chemicals, which results in different health issues for them – such as eye damage, lung and respiratory problems, nausea and headaches – as well as environmental problems for the planet in general.

Ghanaians working in Agbogbloshie, a suburb of Accra, Ghana.

Photo: Wikimedia Commons, CC0.

Moreover, experts predict that consumer demand for electronics will only increase in the coming years. Therefore, finding ecological solutions for effective e-waste management is very much needed. If carried out correctly, e-waste management could create viable and sustainable business models in cities such as Accra, improving people's lives through the generation of employment and environmental protection. Recyclable materials in e-waste can be valuable secondary resources that should be taken into consideration; and the toxic parts that cannot be recycled need to be taken care of by proper handling systems as well (Baldé, 2015).

***

2.5 Urban Land Use and Loss of Green Spaces

Urbanization is one of the predominant issues that is constantly linked to the destruction of green spaces. In most cases, urban growth reduces open and green spaces in and around cities, affecting biodiversity and altering urban ecosystems.

Urban green spaces are parks and gardens that are found inside a city. The importance of these urban green spaces for human well-being and quality of life has been gaining recognition in the past few decades (Gairola and Noresah, 2010). Several studies have found that **living in a "green" environment and/or close to accessible green spaces is important for residents' satisfaction with their living environment, since it increases air quality, facilitates physical exercise and improves mental health.**

The WHO suggests that every city should have a minimum of 9 m^2 of green space per capita and that all residents should live within a 15-minute walk of a green space (UN-Habitat, CBD & UN-Women, 2016). However, the quantity of green space that exists in a city, gauged against its population, varies widely from one city to another. (See Figure 11.) As this issue is deeply connected to urban planning, it will be analyzed further in the volume *Urban Planning* in this series.

Figure 11: Square meters (m^2) of green space in selected cities

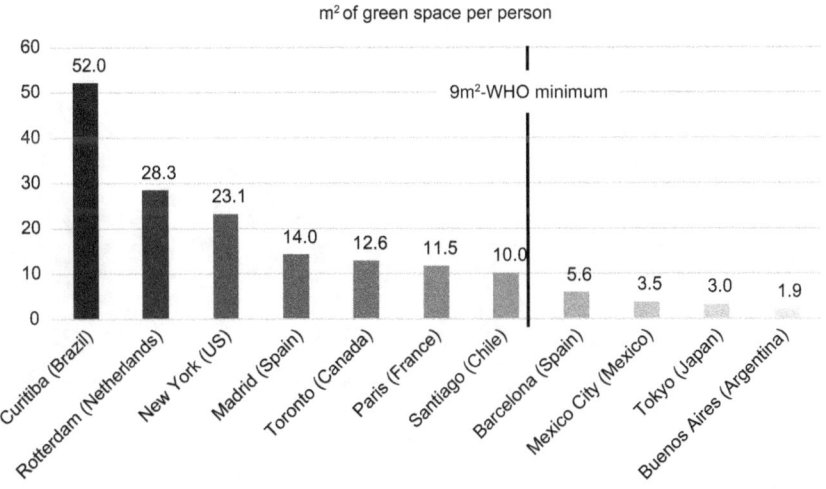

m^2 of green space per person

9m^2-WHO minimum

Source: Prepared by the authors based on Vázquez, 2011.

***

Responding to all these environmental challenges faced by cities will require a well-rounded approach. Some local administrations are making noteworthy improvements, introducing sustainable policies to tackle climate change within urban areas, but more needs to be done. Some of the smart solutions and best practices that are being implemented to diminish the strain on the environment are exhibited in the following section.

***

3. Sustainable and Resilient Futures for Cities: Smart Solutions and Best Practices

An energy-efficient, environmentally friendly and sustainable city ideally should combine economic growth with social equity and a minimum of waste production and GHG emissions (UN-Habitat, 2008b). The main challenge for cities is therefore to implement policies and urban solutions that minimize energy consumption and GHG emissions, that maximize and reuse energy, water and materials and that reduce the vulnerability of urban populations.

Advances in technology and innovation are key both to finding alternative energy options that are cost-efficient and to optimizing energy use. For instance, it is estimated that ICT-enabled solutions have the potential to reduce annual emissions by some 9.1 gigatons (billion tons) of carbon dioxide equivalent ($GtCO_2$) by 2020, representing 16.5% of the projected total in 2020 (GeSI and BCG, 2012). Besides, as we will see in the different best practices presented in this section, policies, legislation and regulations can also play a very important role in shaping and facilitating the market toward the green economy and the clean energy sector. Additionally, the change in people's behavior and preferences, with people more and more concerned about their impact on the planet, is also having a critical impact on the new solutions that are being developed and implemented. Lastly, infrastructure, urban planning and urban form are also very important drivers for implementing smart and sustainable solutions to tackle cities' environmental challenges. All of these different levers of change play and will continue to play a very important role in the current and future management of cities.

Figure 12. Smart urban management model

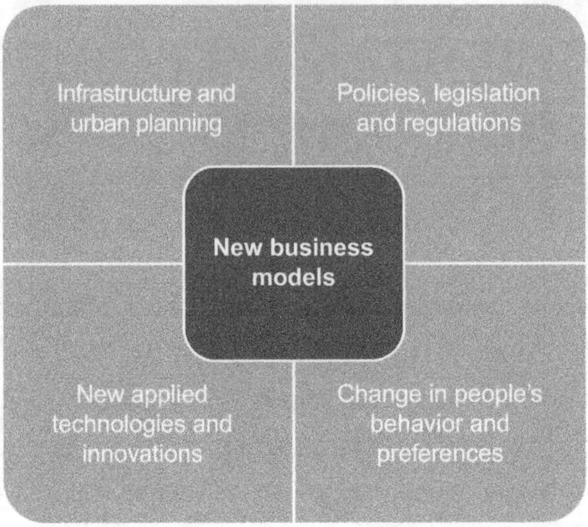

Infrastructure and urban planning	Policies, legislation and regulations
New business models	
New applied technologies and innovations	Change in people's behavior and preferences

Source: Prepared by the authors

At IESE Cities in Motion we have defined a framework of analysis (see Figure 12) with these main leverages of change to help us understand and analyze how they interact with each other in the different solutions created and implemented in the different dimensions.

This section will analyze some examples of international best practices and case studies to promote sustainable urban futures. The different best practices are organized under three main broad themes: (1) environmental governance, (2) environmental urban management, and (3) the green economy and the clean energy sector. For each solution the main leverages of change that play a critical role for that particular best practice will be highlighted in the case study.

Among the different solutions that will be set out, it is important to stress that cities should include solutions and policies for smarter energy – that is, to move from the current unsustainable energy generation based on fossil fuels toward renewable, "clean" fuels and low-carbon energy sources –

and, at the same time, to reduce energy consumption and enhance the efficiency of resource use (e.g., reuse, recycling, green buildings, street lighting and waste management).

Lastly, solutions in two additional dimensions can also have a substantial impact on the environment. First, urban solutions related to transport systems – that is, investment in public transport, clean vehicles, and the promotion of alternatives modes of mobility – can significantly reduce the strain on the environment. And second, urban planning concerns – such as more compact urban forms and connected infrastructure – can also reduce energy use and have a positive impact on the environment. However, these solutions are examined in the volumes *Mobility and Transportation* and *Urban Planning*, respectively, in the series.

***

3.1 Environmental Governance

Environmental governance refers to the means by which society determines and acts on goals and priorities related to the management of natural resources and the environment (IUCN, 2014). Different multilevel actors are involved in the decision-making processes of environmental governance: governments (local, national and international), enterprises and civil society. This section will focus on local governments and on what can they do.

Cities should include sustainability as part of their global city project in a more extensive and comprehensive manner. The inclusion of a comprehensive green action plan as part of the city project is key to achieving this goal, and city managers and local authorities play an important role in this matter.

Policies, legislation and regulations

BEST PRACTICE: VANCOUVER
– the challenge of becoming the greenest city

Vancouver is a coastal seaport city in the southwest corner of British Columbia in Canada. The City of Vancouver is one of 23 local authorities that comprise the region of Metro Vancouver. The greater Vancouver region is the third most populous metropolitan area in the country with almost 2.5 million inhabitants (some 600,000 in the city) in 2,878 km² (metro area). Port Metro Vancouver is one of the busiest and largest ports in Canada. Moreover, Vancouver is one of the most ethnically and linguistically diverse cities in Canada.

The City of Vancouver, Canada

Source: Pixabay, CC0.

Context

- Vancouver is a low-lying coastal, river delta city. With the threat of rising sea levels due to climate change, the city is vulnerable to adverse conditions.

- Vancouver is a high-income city and is considered one of the most livable cities in the world.

Actions

- In 2009, Vancouver mayor Gregor Robertson launched an initiative with the aim of making the city the greenest in the world by 2020.

- To define the strategy, Robertson formed the Greenest City action team, with 16 expert members. They also created a website to receive comments and suggestions from residents.

- After much consultation, in 2010 the Greenest City team, taking into account the ideas from members of the community, defined the Greenest City 2020 Action Plan. The plan was adopted in 2011, containing some 125 projects.

- The plan included different areas and initiatives to address Vancouver's environmental challenges. All these initiatives could be grouped into three main areas for improvement or three high-level objectives: zero carbon, zero waste and healthy ecosystems.

- Moreover, the plan was divided into 10 goals, each with one or more measurable targets to be reached within the following 10 years. These involved growing the green economy (i.e., doubling the number of "green jobs" over 2010 levels by 2020); leading on greenhouse gas reduction (i.e., reducing GHG emissions by 33% from 2007 levels); zero waste (i.e., reducing total

Greenest City framework

ZERO CARBON	Climate Leadership		
	Green Transportation		
	Green Buildings		
ZERO WASTE	Zero Waste	Green Economy	Lighter Footprint
HEALTHY ECOSYSTEMS	Access to Nature		
	Clean Water		
	Local Food		
	Clean Air		

Source: City of Vancouver, 2015.

solid waste going to landfills or incinerators by 50% from 2008 levels); creating green buildings; green transportation options; providing access to nature; reducing the city's carbon footprint; providing clean water and providing clean air and local food (City of Vancouver, 2012).

- There was no official budget to support the Greenest City 2020 Action Plan, but the City of Vancouver and the Vancouver Foundation created a fund, the Greenest City Fund, with a budget of C$2 million for a period of four years (Berrone et al., 2014).

Outcomes

- According to the City of Vancouver, significant progress has been made. As of the end of 2014, GHG emissions had decreased by 7% since 2007, with a 5% reduction in community building CO_2 emissions.

- Moreover, by 2014 the total vehicle kilometers driven per person had decreased by 21% since 2007; by 2013 the tons of waste to landfill or incinerators had fallen by 18% since 2008; the number of green jobs increased by 19% in the period from 2010 to 2013; and 37,000 new trees had been planted since 2010; among other improvements (City of Vancouver, 2015).

- The plan has been shown as an example of best practice in the field and has received international recognition with several awards, such as being named the Global Earth Hour Capital 2013 in the WWF's Earth Hour City Challenge, or achieving the second position in the U.S. and Canada Green City Index 2011, a research project conducted by the Economist Intelligence Unit and Siemens.

- In March 2015, Vancouver City Council took its commitment to a renewable future beyond 2020 to 2050 with the Renewable City Strategy. As part of this plan, the city has committed itself to run on 100% renewable energy before 2050, including electricity, cooling and housing. As of 2015, the amount of Vancouver's energy derived from renewable sources was already 31%.

- As part of its Greenest City Action Plan, the renewable city goals will rely on collaboration with business, government and the public.

- However, the project has received some criticism. Some criticized it for not providing a cost analysis (Berrone et al., 2014). Others criticized the difficulty of setting measurable targets or a lack of clarity and focus on the big picture. It is probably too soon to assess the failure or success of the project.

***

Change in people's behavior and preferences

Policies, legislation and regulations

BEST PRACTICE: COPENHAGEN
— the first capital to become carbon-neutral

Copenhagen is the capital and the most populated city of Denmark. Situated on the eastern coast of Zealand, the city has 1,246,611 inhabitants (2014) in an area of 86.2 km². The metropolitan area has almost two million people. Copenhagen is the economic and financial center of Denmark, with the service sector being the most important one, especially transport and communications, trade and finance. Nationally, its GDP per capita ranks Denmark in the top

Copenhagen, Denmark

Source: Pixabay, CC0.

10 countries in the world and the country is one of the 15 most competitive economies globally (Floater et al., 2014).

Context

- Copenhagen is an environmentally friendly city that has been widely recog-
  nized as a green economy leader.

- At an international level, Copenhagen always ranks very high for quality of life,
  innovation and competitiveness (Floater et al., 2014).

Actions

- In 2011, building on the city council's previous commitment to an action plan
  against climate change in 2009, the Danish capital set the goal of becoming
  the world's first carbon-neutral capital city by 2025. To meet this ambitious
  goal, in 2012 the council adopted a comprehensive carbon reduction master
  plan, the so-called CPH 2025 Climate Plan.

- The plan aims to complement and coordinate the objectives of several other
  existing policy frameworks in energy, transportation, development planning,
  and waste. The CPH 2025 Climate Plan is organized on the basis of four pil-
  lars: energy consumption, energy production, green mobility, and city administration. It is a comprehensive plan on sustainability and the environment.

- The plan's major goals for 2025 in energy consump-tion: 20% reduction in heat consumption, 20% reduction in electricity consumption in commercial and service com-panies and 10% reduction in electricity consumption in households (all compared with 2010 levels), and installation of solar cells corresponding to 1% of electricity consumption (City of Copenhagen, 2012).

Distribution of total CO_2 reduction by 2025

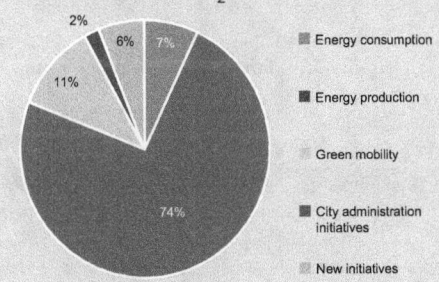

Source: Prepared by the authors based on City of Copenhagen, 2012.

- As part of the master plan, the city aims to reduce the city's CO_2 consumption
  levels from around 2.5 million tons in 2009 to under 1.2 million tons by 2025.

- The plan also includes major goals for energy production: the city aims to make district heating and cooling carbon neutral, achieve electricity production based on wind and biomass, separate the plastic waste from households and business, and achieve the biogasification of organic waste (City of Copenhagen, 2012). The plan aims to replace coal with biomass as the primary fuel for the city's combined heat and power generation plants.

- The plan is also focused on mobility. It aims to eliminate fossil fuels from transport and promote the use of public transport, walking and multimodal trips. Another aim of the plan is that 75% of all trips in Copenhagen will be by bicycle, on foot or by public transport by 2025 (and that 50% of trips to work or school will be by bike, up from the average of 36% for the period from 2008 to 2010).

- The project has taken an interdisciplinary approach with close collaboration with business and knowledge institutions.

- The municipality plans to invest approximately 2.7 billion Danish kroner (around $400 million) by 2025. This amount and private investment are estimated to reach up to $4.78 billion over the same period (Gerdes, 2013).

Outcomes

- In 2011, Copenhagen had reduced CO_2 emissions by 21% compared with the 2005 level. By 2011, CO_2 emissions in Copenhagen were approximately 1.9 million tons. With these levels it is not difficult to imagine that the city will achieve its goal of reducing CO_2 emissions to 1.2 million tons by 2025 (City of Copenhagen, 2012).

- In 2011, energy savings accounted for nearly 7% of the total CO_2 reduction, energy production initiatives for 74%, and transport initiatives for 11%.

- By 2025, the city expects commercial buildings to lower energy consumption by 20%, households by 10%, and public buildings by 40%.

- It is estimated that by 2025 a couple with one child and one car living in an apartment could save approximately 6,500 kroner per year (City of Copenhagen, 2012).

- The project expects to improve Copenhagen residents' quality of life as well as foster green economic growth.

- According to the Siemens European Green City Index, the city of Copenhagen ranks as the most sustainable city in Europe.

- Finally, these investments in the green economy are expected to have significant effects on employment. The eventual outcome on the economy will be seen in the years to come.

3.2 Environmental Urban Management

The challenges related to environmental urban management are many and diverse: low coverage and poor quality of basic services; increased demand for water and problems in delivering it efficiently; inefficient waste collection and management, etc. This section will cover some examples of international best practices and smart solutions regarding environmental urban management.

3.2.1 Sustainable Land Use Policies

The enhancement of sustainable land use policies – such as the promotion of pedestrian-friendly neighborhoods, cycle lanes, a compact higher-density urban form, more green spaces and parks (see Box 4), and reduced urban sprawl – are much needed for effective environmental urban management.[5]

A park in London, UK

Source: Pixabay, CC0.

---

[5] These issues will be analyzed further in the volumes *Mobility and Transportation and Urban Planning* in this series.

Infrastructure and urban planning

BOX 4: How can green spaces be increased in cities when there is no space left? Pocket parks!

Urbanization usually goes hand in hand with a reduction in green spaces and open spaces. Nevertheless, some cities have found an interesting strategic solution to increase green spaces where there is no free space left for them: pocket parks. Pocket parks are open urban spaces on a very small scale, usually only a few house lots in size or smaller (Blake, n.d.). They are usually between or behind a couple of apartment blocks.

Pocket parks or mini parks can include spaces for relaxing, a playground for children, a small place for events, a small café, etc., and they are relatively manageable (Dimitriadi, 2013). In fact, in many cases they are community-based projects that not only contribute to a better environment but also create a stronger feeling of community. Moreover, they make use of a "forgotten space" that otherwise would not be used for anything. Some examples of cities incorporating pocket parks in their urban planning are New York, Copenhagen, Sydney or Mexico City, among many others

Parley Park: a pocket park in Manhattan, New York City

Source: Jim Henderson — Wikimedia Commons.

3.2.2 Water Management

The efficient distribution and use of water are essential for urban development. As seen in Section 2, one of the main challenges affecting the sustainability of human urban settlements is the lack of access to safe water and sanitation. Therefore, city administrations around the world should put their efforts into areas such as water treatment and wastewater recycling, resource recovery and pollution control, as well as initiatives to reduce water consumption.

However, it is important to mention that the challenges faced by cities in developing countries differ greatly from the ones of cities in developed countries, since developing countries are much more lacking in basic infrastructure and services.

Policies, legislation and regulations

New applied technologies and innovations

BEST PRACTICE: NEWater
– solving **SINGAPORE's** water problem by purifying used water

Singapore is a city-state in Southeast Asia. It hosts some 5.4 million inhabitants (2014) in an area covering approximately 700 km^2, comprising 63 small islands. Founded as a British trade colony in 1819, since its independence in 1965 it has become one of the world's most prosperous cities, with GDP of US$308.05 billion and GDP per capita of US$56,319. Moreover, it has the most active port in the world.

Singapore

Source: Pixabay, CC0.

Context

- Since the city gained independence in 1965, lack of water has been a critical issue for Singapore.

- Singapore has a natural rainforest climate and an average annual rainfall of 2,300 to 2,400 mm. However, the city-state has faced persistent water shortages throughout its history, since it lacks natural freshwater lakes.

- Singapore's average water demand in 2010 was 1.4 million cubic meters per day.

- Approximately half of Singapore's water is imported from Malaysia.

- The World Resources Institute classed Singapore as in the "extreme" category of water stress, at the level of states such as Saudi Arabia and Kuwait (Mao, 2014).

- The leaders of the city-state have made water security a top priority: they needed to diversify their sources to be able to meet Singapore's demand for water.

Actions

- Singapore's first water master plan dates back decades. In 1974, the Public Utilities Board (PUB) built a pilot plant, which was a precursor of today's NEWater Factory, to transform treated used water into drinking water. However, the costs were too high.

- In 1998, the Singapore Water Reclamation Study (NEWater Study) began as a joint initiative between PUB and the Ministry of the Environment and Water Resources (MEWR). The first NEWater plant was completed in 2000 and has been operating since 2003 (PUB, 2014; Mao, 2014).

- In 2002, the NEWater program was created with the aim of providing a sustainable water source for Singapore's population.

- By March 2014, there were four NEWater plants in Singapore (PUB, 2014).

- NEWater is high-grade reclaimed water produced from treated used water that is further purified using advanced membrane technology (microfiltration and reverse osmosis) and ultraviolet disinfection, making it clean and safe to drink. NEWater has passed more than 130,000 scientific tests and exceeds the drinking water standards set by the WHO and the U.S. Environmental Protection Agency.

- NEWater is used primarily for nonpotable industrial purposes.

- Since the public was not convinced that NEWater water was safe for consumption, an effective public communications plan was also necessary to convince the population that it was indeed clean and safe and to convince those in industry that it was suitable for their processes (United Nations, 2014).

Outcomes

- In the past 30 years, Singapore policy makers significantly strengthened the city-state's internal capacities, reducing its dependence on outside sources for water. The city has not only been successful in becoming self-sufficient in terms of water supply but it has also managed to transform this area of vulnerability into an opportunity (Euricur et al., 2014).

- The NEWater program is a good example of best practice for innovative water management and it has gained international recognition, winning several awards such as the Stockholm Industry Water Award in 2007 and the "Water for Life" UN-Water Best Practices Award in 2014.

Singapore's "Four National Taps"

Source: Nanyang Technological University, 2014.

- Now Singapore has four different sources of water supply or water solutions, known as the "Four National Taps": water from local catchment areas, imported water, reclaimed water known as NEWater and desalinated water (PUB, 2014). This is part of a long-term water supply strategy that has allowed for a diversified and sustainable water supply.

- Moreover, thanks to effective water treatment processes and continued investment in R&D, Singapore's tap water is of good quality and complies with the WHO's drinking water guidelines, being suitable for drinking without any further filtration.

- Currently, NEWater meets up to 30% of Singapore's current water demand, which stands at about 1.5 billion liters a day (PUB, 2014; United Nations, 2014).

- Since the resulting water from NEWater is ultrapure water, it is not used for domestic use but is used by industry, such as in water fabrication processes. However, according to the Singaporean authorities, although it is not supplied directly to households it would be safe to drink it directly.

- In order to be self-sufficient, the government of Singapore aims by 2060 to acquire 50% of water resources from reclaimed water using the NEWater project, 30% from seawater desalination and 20% from rainfall collected in water catchment areas (Mao, 2014).

- The Singapore government announced in 2011 it would invest about S$330 million in water R&D over five years (PUB, 2014). As a result of this investment in R&D and new technologies, the water sector was expected to grow from S$500 million in 2003 (0.3% of GDP) to S$1.7 billion (0.6% of GDP) by 2015 and jobs in the sector were expected to double to about 11,000 jobs by 2015 (Euricur et al., 2014; Mao, 2014).

- Moreover, as a consequence of this investment and the economic growth relating to the water sector, Singapore has positioned itself as a "global hydro-hub" for water technologies, hosting around 130 local and international water companies and 26 research institutes (Euricur et al., 2014).

***

3.2.3 Waste Management Systems

Cities have the challenge of providing an effective and efficient waste management system to their residents. It is important that city administrations around the world approach the problem in a comprehensive manner and put in place strategies and programs to reduce, reuse, recycle and/or recover as much waste as possible and that these are unified in an integrated, well-managed solid waste plan.

In fact, cities could make important cost-effective investments in waste-related GHG emissions that could bring at the same time economic and climate benefits, such as recycling, landfill gas capture or the enhanced composting of waste. Yet in some cases, especially in rapidly expanding developing cities, this is no easy task, since they have to deal with high growth rates of municipal solid waste generation and tight budgets and resources. To give just one example, the Indian city of Kolkata could cut its waste-related GHG emissions by 41% by 2025 through investments

New business models

BOX 5: Oslo, the city that is so clean it imports waste to burn

Oslo, the capital of Norway, is known as being one of the top sustainable cities in the world. Among its policies and regulations, the city of Oslo is committed to reducing its GHG emissions by 50% by 2030, to investing in the development of new technologies for renewable energies, and to energy recovery.

In fact, the Scandinavian city, with high recycling rates, became so efficient in energy recovery – generating energy by burning waste in huge incinerators – that it began running out of trash. Some years ago, Oslo started importing garbage from other places, such as the United Kingdom and the Republic of Ireland in order to be able to cope with the shortage of garbage for meeting the city's energy needs. Today, approximately half of Oslo's households and buildings are heated by energy generated from waste incineration from the city's waste-to-energy plants.

of 13.1 billion rupees ($224 million in 2014) (New Climate Economy, 2014). However, sometimes these investments are just too much for some municipal budgets.

Other cities, however, are showing promising and ambitious plans to deal with waste management systems and reduce waste-related GHG emissions. For instance, the U.S. city of San Francisco in California has a goal of "zero waste" by 2020, through increasing access to recycling or composting. In fact, the city has already exceeded its goal of diverting 75% of materials away from landfills by 2010 (SF Environment, 2015).

Moreover, new technological breakthroughs can be of substantial help in improving today's urban waste management situation. For instance, existing technologies allow us to capture and flare methane emissions from landfills and use these to generate electricity (Mutizwa-Mangiza et al., 2011). However, again, many developing countries still lack this technology for methane recuperation.

BEST PRACTICE: BELO HORIZONTE
— solid waste management

New applied technologies and innovations

Belo Horizonte is the capital of the state of Minas Gerais in the southeast of Brazil and is the country's first planned city. It is the sixth most populous city in the country, with 2,491,109 inhabitants (2014) in an area of some 330 km², including around half a million living in favelas. Its metropolitan area is the third largest in Brazil, with more than five million people. In 2012, Belo Horizonte's GDP per capita was US$17,239, placing it seventh among the 13 Brazilian metropolitan areas.

Belo Horizonte, Brazil

Source: Pixabay, CC0.

Context

- With rapid urbanization and growing levels of disposable income, urban dwellers were producing more waste than ever before. Most low and middle-income cities dispose of their waste in open dumps and some have poorly operated landfills.

- Belo Horizonte produces some 3,500 tons of municipal solid waste every day and an average of 0.7 kg of waste per capita (Oliveira de Medeiros, 2012; Rode and Floater, 2013).

- Belo Horizonte has a strong and extensive development of solid waste management initiatives, such as the Integrated Solid Waste Management Model of 1993, implementing recycling programs and selective collection (UN-Habitat, 2010).

- The Municipal Department of Urban Cleaning (Superintendência de Limpeza Urbana or SLU) is responsible for municipal waste management.

- From 1975 to 2007 all municipal solid waste from Belo Horizonte went to a disposal site (called CTRS BR-040) 12 kilometers from the city center (UN-Habitat,

2010). However, at the end of the 1990s and beginning of the 2000s, the landfill was approaching its maximum capacity. Toward the end of 2006, more than 17.4 million cubic meters of waste had been deposited in the landfill (Oliveira de Medeiros, 2012).

- Solid waste is a large source of methane, a potent GHG, and when uncollected it contributes to flooding and air pollution and affects public health. The landfill site used to be one of the highest contributors to GHG emissions in Belo Horizonte.

Actions

- In 2006, the Municipal Department for the Environment established the Municipal Committee on Climate Change and Eco-Efficiency (Comitê Municipal sobre Mudanças Climáticas e Ecoeficiência or CMMCE), including different stakeholders from the municipal and state government, civil society, nongovernmental organizations, the private sector and academia (UN-Habitat, 2010). The committee introduced the Municipal Policy for Climate Change Mitigation, including a target of reducing GHG emissions by 20% by the year 2030 compared with 2007 levels.

Landfill site CTRS BR-040 in Belo Horizonte, Brazil

Source: Imagery © 2016 Google, DigitalGlobe.

- In December 2007 the landfill was closed. However, the city needed to find solutions: first, in order to manage the municipal solid waste; and second, to decide what to do with the landfill site, which remained a burden on the quality of life of the local people and environment (Oliveira de Medeiros, 2012).

- A waste-to-energy approach for the landfill was identified. In particular, the landfill-related project had the objective of implementing effective landfill site management and reducing GHG emissions by recovering gas from the landfill and generating combustible natural gas. With this solution it was possible to address the existing environmental challenges, as well as contribute to the city's growing energy demands.

- Belo Horizonte's politicians and technicians envisioned the potential to capture landfill gas with new technologies and in 2007 the local government launched a tender process, seeking a specialist company to capture the landfill biogas (Oliveira de Medeiros, 2012). The tender was granted to the Italian company Asja Ambiente Italia SpA, which had to collect, treat and transmit the biogas generated at the CTRS BR-040 landfill.

- Moreover, the city government has also introduced several programs for improving and increasing recycling, including the informal sector in municipal recycling strategies. The main focus has been on developing partnerships between the SLU and local waste pickers' cooperatives in order to increase recycling rates, social inclusion, job creation and income generation (Rode and Floater, 2013).

Outcomes and lessons

- In 2010, the plant became fully operational. In 2011, it had a gross electricity production of 30,400 MWh. After discounting the energy the biogas plant consumed for maintenance and operation, it supplied some 28,000 MWh of electricity to Belo Horizonte's electricity grid or, in other words, enough electricity for 30,000 to 35,000 people (Oliveira de Medeiros, 2012).

- The GHG emissions from the landfill have been cut significantly since 2009.

- Although more desirable waste management practices should be considered first – such as reducing, reusing and recycling – waste for energy production can also be a resourceful option for a city.

- Additionally, while recycling rates until 2009 remained relatively low at around 5% to 7% of total waste, the city has made significant advances in recent years through the different programs already mentioned (Rode and Floater, 2013).

- In the case study of Belo Horizonte, the key achievements of producing energy from landfill methane could be summarized as follows: (a) additional energy generation, reducing dependency on fossil fuels; (b) reductions in GHG emissions, improving the city's carbon footprint; and (c) improving the environmental and social conditions of people living near the landfill. (Complaints from residents have fallen significantly.)

- Belo Horizonte's approach to waste management is characterized by a strong emphasis on local partnerships. Local governments can provide regulation, guidance and training to waste producers and work with relevant stakeholders to establish effective solutions (Oliveira de Medeiros, 2012). In the case of

Belo Horizonte, the local administrations came up with the solutions and initiated the projects but the investment and running of the landfill project were outsourced to a private enterprise and the recycling initiative handed to the waste pickers' cooperatives.

***

3.3 The Green Economy and the Clean Energy Sector

The objective of achieving a sustainable urban system can not only reduce environmental risks and improve human well-being and quality of life but it can also be economically beneficial. In fact, **environmental benefits can go hand in hand with economic benefits**, as will be shown in this section.

Figure 13: Environmental performance vs. gross value added (GVA) per capita in 2009

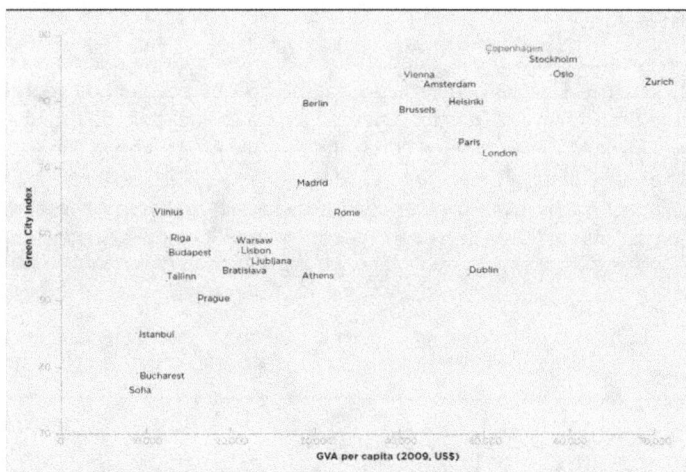

Source: Floater et al., 2014, based on Brookings Institution, LSE Cities and Deutsche Bank Research (2010), Global Metro Monitor: The Path to Economic Recovery, Washington, D.C., and London; Siemens, 2009.

Note: The green index is based on Siemens' 2009 European Green City Index, and GVA per capita in 2009.

The green economy and the clean energy sector cover various areas from renewable energies to energy efficiency and energy savings through intelligent smart energy systems (smart grids), green buildings and public lighting, and they can be an important source of economic growth. (See Box 6.)

BOX 6: Green innovation as a driver of economic growth for cities

Promotion of a green economy and the development of a clean-tech sector in a city can be a powerful catalyst for the local economy and a source of employment. The clean energy sector and the green economy have grown rapidly in recent years, with investments in renewables up to $270 billion and in energy efficiency of at least $130 billion (New Climate Economy, 2015).

These developments are mostly down to the private sector. However, in many cases, market failures reduce the incentives to invest in green innovation, since the returns are usually long-term. In fact, sometimes the returns are higher in socioeconomic and environmental terms for the residents than for the firms (Floater et al., 2013; Thiagarajan, 2015). Therefore, the role of local administrations in correcting these market failures and creating some form of public-private partnership can be crucial.

Some examples of specific support for green technology research in cities are: Stockholm's Electrum Foundation, established by several key representatives from Stockholm's ICT sector (Ericsson, IBM and PacketFront) together with the Royal Institute of Technology (KTH) and the City of Stockholm (Floater et al., 2013); the Copenhagen Clean-Tech Cluster, started in 2009 as a partner-based project launched by Danish clean-tech companies, research institutions and public organizations; Cleantech San Diego; and the Singapore Sustainability Alliance.

***

3.3.1 Renewable Energy Sources

Renewable energy technologies have existed for decades but the prices were just too high. Only hydropower was used on a large scale. However, its important effects on the ecosystem in which the hydro plant is placed have made this low-carbon technology very controversial. But in the past few years some renewable energy sources have gone from prohibitively expensive to realistic as options. For instance, **wind power** is one-third cheaper than 25 years ago and **solar power** costs have fallen by half since 2010, and they are now viable large-scale options. Other renewable energy options besides solar energy and wind energy are **biomass and biofuel.**

Figure 14: Costs of solar PV electricity over time

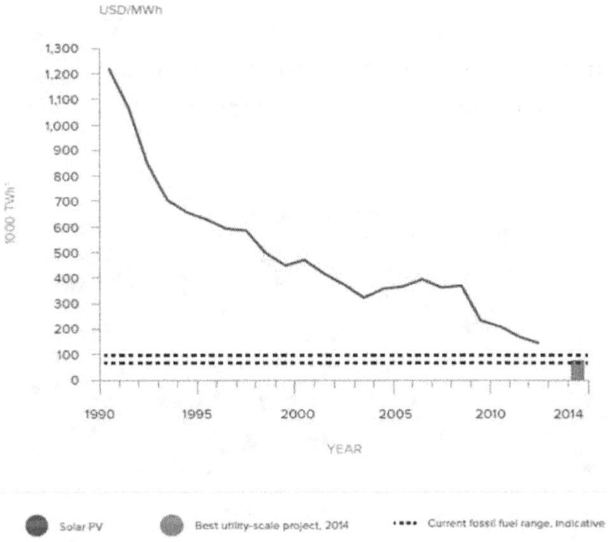

Source: New Climate Economy, 2014.

But it was not only the falling costs of these types of energy that led to increased interest in renewables. It was also because of the fact that they can strengthen energy security, reducing the dependence on fossil fuels and exposure to global market volatility (New Climate Economy, 2014). Moreover, recent technological advances have allowed the use of ICT to help reduce the variability of wind and solar power production, making these clean sources of energy more attractive and successful options.

Despite falling prices and the great advantages of renewables, on a larger scale, sometimes they still require political will and public support. (See the panel Best Practice: Barcelona.) Nonetheless, public support has to be gathered correctly, because when this is done badly it can alter and mislead the market.

Lastly, it is important to mention that many people still have no access to energy such as electricity, especially in slums and informal settlements in rapidly growing developing cities. **Renewables could be a good option to complement other sources of energy to overcome barriers to access for people living in developing cities, without repeating the mistakes of developed cities.**

New applied technologies and innovations

Policies, legislation and regulations

BEST PRACTICE: BARCELONA
— solar energy

Barcelona is the most populous city of Catalonia and the second most populous of Spain. It has 1,602,386 inhabitants (2014) in an area of 101 km², with a density of 15,800 inhabitants per square kilometer (Idescat, 2015). The city is also the center of one of the Mediterranean coast's largest metropolitan areas, with around five million inhabitants in an area of 4,268 km². Barcelona is a major economic center with one of the most important European ports in the Mediterranean Sea. In 2010, Barcelona's GDP was €61.9 billion, representing 30.2% of Catalonia's total, while the GDP per capita

Barcelona, Spain

Source: Pixabay, CC0.

was €38,500 (Barcelona Activa, 2014). The city is also an important cultural center, particularly known for its architecture, and a major tourist destination, with around 7.8 million visitors in 2014.

Context

- Barcelona has an average of 2,800 hours of sunshine per year, making it suitable for solar power (NYC Global Partners, 2011c).

- With high levels of energy consumption, Barcelona City Council aimed to promote energy efficiency and the use of renewable energy sources.

Actions

- In order to mitigate climate change and reduce energy consumption and GHG emissions, Barcelona became the first European city to have a solar thermal ordinance (STO). The ordinance was approved in July 1999 and came into effect in August 2000.

- The ordinance makes it compulsory to use solar energy to supply 60% of running hot water in all new buildings, renovated buildings or buildings that change their use. The ordinance applies to both private and public buildings and to all commercial and residential buildings with more than 16 apartments.

- Since 2000, various improvements to and amendments of the initial plan have been introduced, including the transformation of municipal buildings so they use photovoltaic (PV) energy and the development of self-sufficient solar-powered bus stops (NYC Global Partners, 2011c).

- In 2002, the city established the Barcelona Local Energy Agency and the first Energy Improvement Plan, with a set of 55 strategies, from energy conservation to education programs, in order to promote energy efficiency and renewable energy (Caamaño-Martín, 2008; Guevara-Stone, 2014). The Barcelona Energy Action is responsible for implementing, monitoring and disseminating the ordinance.

- Many actions were taken during the whole process including: stakeholder engagement (a working group called Taula Solar was created with different professionals and associations from related sectors to support debate), capacity building (Barcelona City Council staff were given training on solar energy), information campaigns and fiscal incentives (the Municipal Fiscal Ordinance set out discounts in housing taxes for voluntary solar energy) (Marques and Pujol, 2014).

- In 2004, as part of the Universal Forum of Cultures, a large pergola structure with solar panels was built. The structure has a surface covering 10,500 m² (the largest PV array in Europe at that time) that captures solar energy and delivers it to the public electrical grid (NYC Global Partners, 2011c).

- In 2006, the ordinance was amended to expand the scope of the buildings to which it applies, by including smaller buildings, and to add technical requirements. The so-called Barnamil Campaign involves installing solar panels for heating domestic water in urban residential areas (UN-Habitat, 2008a).

- In 2007, a municipal building was built with a solar cooling plant and, by the end of 2008, 39 public buildings had installed solar cells.

- In 2009, the Barcelona Transport Authority introduced 2,000 solar-powered bus stops in 18 municipalities in the Barcelona metropolitan area, which are self-sufficient and remarkably energy-efficient. The solar bus stops were developed by a public-private partnership involving Capmar, S.L., and the Istituto Europeo di Design in Barcelona (Marques and Pujol, 2014; NYC Global Partners, 2011c).

- In 2011, the city council approved the Barcelona Energy, Climate Change and Air Quality Plan 2011–2020. The plan contains 108 projects that focus on improving technology, raising awareness, and managing energy demand (Marques and Pujol, 2014).

Photovoltaic pergola at the Universal Forum of Cultures

Source: Wikimedia Commons.

- The costs of the mandatory installation of solar thermal heaters in private buildings are borne by the private sector (with fiscal incentives) and the municipal solar thermal installations were carried out by Barcelona City Council.

Outcomes

- The total surface area of installed solar panels increased from 1,650 m² in 2000 to 87,600 m² in 2010 (Marques and Pujol, 2014).

- This has created projected energy savings of more than 11,200 MWh each year and a reduction in GHG emissions of some 1,970 tons of CO_2 per year (Marques and Pujol, 2014). The abovementioned pergola alone produces 554 MWh of power per year, reducing the city's carbon emissions by 440 tons per year (Guevara-Stone, 2014).

- The 2006 amended ordinance helped Barcelona reduce the carbon intensity of its electricity by about 30%.

- However, in 2010 only 46% of the total area approved for solar thermal infra-structure had been provided with the systems, and only 20% of all the systems were operational, mainly due to the negative perception of different stake-holders (Marques and Pujol, 2014).

- Close collaboration, capacity building and information dissemination have been found to be essential for the success of the strategy.

- It is important to mention that the ordinance was prepared and implemented thanks to the political will of the local administration to promote solar energy. Before the local government intervened and took a leading role, the solar thermal market remained underdeveloped (Marques and Pujol, 2014). There-fore, city governments can indeed be very influential and make a difference.

- In 2002, the project won Barcelona the European Climate Star, awarded by Climate Alliance.

- Barcelona's successful model inspired other cities and it has been replicated in other cities in Spain (with more than 70 Spanish municipalities adopting solar ordinances afterwards) and in other European cities.

***

3.3.2 Energy Efficiency

Along with the use of renewable energies and materials, energy efficiency is a crucial factor in light of increasing energy demand and limited resources. Energy efficiency is understood as using less energy to provide the same product or service. For instance, by insulating a home and allowing a building to use less heating and cooling energy to achieve comfortable temperatures, or by using more efficient household appliances and compact fluorescent lights that last longer and consume less.

But energy efficiency has benefits that go beyond reductions in energy demand and energy consumption. It also helps economic growth, enhances social development, advances environmental sustainability and ensures energy security (IEA, 2014a). For instance, according to the International Energy Agency (IEA), an additional dollar spent on more efficient electrical equipment, appliances and buildings saves more than $2 in investment in electricity supply (IEA, 2006b).

New business models

BOX 7: Open District Heating in Stockholm

As part of the European Union's Horizon 2020 growth strategy aimed at fostering smart, sustainable and inclusive growth, the project GrowSmarter was created with the aim of bringing industry and cities together to develop and integrate smart city solutions in the transport, energy and infrastructure sectors. The project's overall objective is to reduce transport emissions and energy usage, as well as to create around 1,500 jobs in the EU.

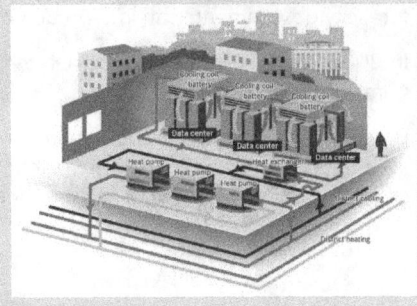

Source: http://www.opendistrictheating.com and http://www.grow-smarter.eu.

One of these solutions is the Open District Heating model, which offers the possibility of recycling energy that otherwise would be wasted. The concept behind this business model is to recover waste heat from places such as data centers, supermarkets and shopping malls with many freezers and coolers that generate large amounts of extra heat and to reuse this extra heat by selling it to other customers needing heat. In this way, this new business model allows for the recovery of waste heat that otherwise would be lost to the atmosphere via cooling towers. According to some estimates, using this model could heat around 100,000 apartments in Stockholm, making the district heating system much more effective and enabling large amounts of energy to be saved.

Globally, about 80% of countries around the world have decreased their energy intensity since 1990 (Enerdata, 2013). However, the potential for further energy efficiency and energy saving is still very high. **The global energy efficiency market is worth at least $310 billion a year and it is expected to keep growing** (IEA, 2014b).

Local and city governments can again be very influential in this regard. They can drive energy-efficiency markets and help improve energy efficiency through energy-efficiency programs and policies that can be adopted at a subnational level.

a. Smart Grids

Technological advances can enhance the effectiveness of grid systems by improving efficiency in day-to-day grid operations. A smart grid is an energy network that can automatically monitor energy flows through smart meters, digital computing power, interconnected communications networks and other strategies and adjust the flows to take account of changes in energy supply and demand according to the behavior and actions of all users connected to the grid (generators and consumers). In this way, smart grids can optimize energy flows and provide consumers and suppliers with real-time information that allows them to reduce energy consumption and increase energy efficiency, ensuring a sustainable, economic and secure energy supply at the same time.

Smart grids can also be very helpful for renewable energies. As the sun does not always shine and the wind does not blow all the time either, merging information on energy demand with weather forecasts could allow grid operators to plan the integration of renewable energy into the grid better. Smart grids can therefore be very effective in helping with the variability and instability of renewables.

Today, utility companies are operating pilot programs in many cities around the world to test the technologies of smart grids.

New applied technologies and innovations

Infrastructure and urban planning

BEST PRACTICE: MÁLAGA
— smart grid

Málaga is a city in the autonomous community of Andalusia, in the south of Spain. The city has some 568,000 inhabitants in an area of 389 km², making it the sixth largest city in Spain. The most important economic sectors of the city are tourism, construction and technology services.

City of Málaga, Spain

Source: Pixabay, CC0.

Context

- In 2007, the European Union established an ambitious energy plan as part of its fight against climate change and in order to enhance energy efficiency. The plan focused on three main goals to be achieved by 2020: reducing greenhouse gases by 20% with respect to 1990 levels; increasing energy efficiency, achieving savings of 20% with respect to the consumption forecast for 2020; and ensuring that 20% of the total energy consumed is from renewable sources (Endesa, 2014).

Actions

- The Smartcity Málaga project started in 2009 with the aim of rationalizing users' energy consumption and cutting CO_2 emissions using new technologies.

- The consortium created to develop the project consists of 11 companies led by Endesa, Spain's leading electricity company, and 14 research institutions.

- The main goals of the project were: improving the grid operation, creating new services and tariff systems for users, improving efficiency, and incorporating renewable energy sources through distributed generation.

- The project consists of modernizing and optimizing the existing electricity grid and does not involve building new networks.

- The use of new smart meters in the context of remote management enables more sustainable electricity consumption.

- The Smartcity Málaga project also aims to achieve greater integration of renewable energy sources into the electricity grid. With this goal in mind, storage systems based on the use of batteries have been introduced to help incorporate renewable energy.

- The area where the project was developed has a population of around 50,000 inhabitants, with 11,000 domestic, 900 commercial and 300 industrial customers.

Outcomes

- The project is one of the Europe's largest eco-efficient city initiatives and forms part of the European Union's 20-20-20 goals. It has served as a "living lab" for future smart grid technologies.

Distribution grid of Smartcity Málaga

- The project aimed to avoid the release of more than 6,000 tons of CO_2 per annum. From its launch in 2009 up to 2013, the project avoided the release into the atmosphere of 4,500 tons of CO_2 per annum, a 20% cut in emissions.

- In its first five years (2009–2013), the Smartcity Málaga project achieved energy savings of 25% in overall electricity consumption in its area.

Source: Endesa, 2014.

- More than 17,000 smart meters have been installed, and a sample of 50 of these users have energy efficiency solutions for the home.

- Eight SMEs and three "emblematic buildings" in the area have had energy-efficiency solutions installed that enable them to monitor consumption and have some control over their electrical charge.

- Cooperation among the partners from distinct disciplines has allowed the concentration of know-how and experience, resulting in benefits for the project.

- Endesa's Smartcity Málaga project won two prizes at the European Smart Metering Awards 2011.

Change in people's behavior and preferences

BOX 8: Envision Charlotte: saving energy by changing behavior

In 2010 the city of Charlotte, in the U.S. state of North Carolina, implemented a new initiative called Envision Charlotte. The initiative is the result of a public-private partnership that covers four main programs: energy, water, air and waste.

Regarding the energy goal, Envision Charlotte aimed to reduce the city's uptown energy consumption by 20% over five years using smart grid technologies.

Charlotte, USA.

Source: Pixabay, CC0.

The idea behind it was not just to use technology per se but to use information provided by technology to change consumers' behavior and encourage energy efficiency. The initiative involved a combination of a digital smart grid and building automation technologies, as well as energy tracking tools, to provide building owners and office workers with near real-time information about the buildings' energy use.

The program was tested on 61 commercial buildings with an area of 10,000 square feet (929 m²) or more in the city's uptown district. Participants could find interactive kiosks in the lobbies that displayed real-time data about that particular building's energy usage and consumption (Vander-Veen, 2015).

Moreover, another program was launched in 2011 as part of the Smart Energy Now initiative in order to teach and encourage office workers to adopt energy-saving behavior. As of 2014, more than 1,500 people had attended training sessions to learn more about energy consumption and develop action plans to implement in their specific office spaces.

Since its inception, the Envision Charlotte program has yielded an 8.4% reduction in energy use among the participating buildings in uptown Charlotte, most of which is related directly to behavioral changes stimulated by data visualization, which reduced energy use by 6.2%. Moreover, according to Envision Charlotte, from the launch of the initiative up to 2014, businesses saved an estimated $10 million or more. Envision Charlotte is a good example of how using information to change behavior can result in energy efficiency and significant energy savings

***

b. Green Buildings

Improving energy efficiency in the building sector is an issue of critical importance. **Buildings are major consumers of energy, water and other resources, while also producing significant amounts of landfill waste and GHG emissions.** As previously mentioned, they are responsible for 35% to 40% of global energy consumption and 20% to 30% of GHG emissions (UNEP, 2011). Moreover, buildings are the sector with the highest potential for CO_2 reduction if action is taken. (See Figure 15.)

Figure 15: Potential CO_2 reduction by sector – World Totals

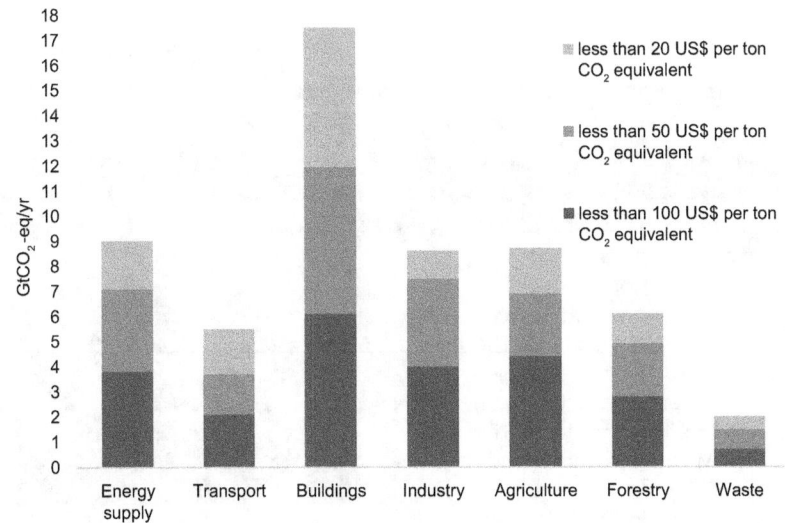

Source: Prepared by the authors based on UNEP, 2011.

Green buildings refer to sustainable buildings — sustainable in both their structure and processes — that are environmentally responsible and resource-efficient throughout the buildings' life cycle from design to construction, operation, maintenance, renovation and deconstruction, in order to minimize the total environmental impact (Build Green, 2011; EPA, 2013).

Smart energy-efficient buildings and materials are cost-efficient, high-value solutions to reduce energy consumption and GHG emissions. **Some strategies and solutions to improve energy efficiency in buildings are: better insulation for cooling and heating, temperature control, automated lighting systems and the use of renewable building materials.** However, sometimes there is a lack of information, technical knowledge and/or capital to invest in energy efficiency, which is an obstacle to increasing the number of energy-efficient buildings or green buildings. Policy makers and other stakeholders need to engage and support green practices and energy efficiency in the building sector in order to move away from current building practices and inefficient energy consumption patterns.

Infrastructure and urban planning

BEST PRACTICE: MELBOURNE
— sustainable buildings

Melbourne is the capital of and the most populous city in the Australian state of Victoria. It is also the second most populous city in Australia and Oceania. The greater metropolitan area of Melbourne covers 9,900 km² with some 4.4 million inhabitants. The City of Melbourne municipality covers 37.7 km² and has a population of around 122,000 (2014)

City of Melbourne

Source: Pixabay, CC0.

(City of Melbourne, 2015b). On an average day, about 805,000 people travel to or are present in the city, and Melbourne hosts more than a million international visitors each year. Economically, Melbourne's GDP is some A\$222 billion and its gross municipal operating budget was A\$355 million (as of 2013) (C40, 2013; Global City Indicators Facility, 2014).

Context

- In the 1980s, Melbourne's city center was almost empty. However, it has experienced incredible growth in the last 20 to 30 years and it is now Australia's fastest-growing city (Cleary and Cotter, 2012). How to manage this growth with limited resources has been critical for the city administration in order to ensure growth that is both economically and environmentally responsible.

- In 2003, Melbourne set the goal of becoming carbon-neutral by 2020. Melbourne's eco-city vision is an overarching plan covering different programs. (Note: this case study covers only the 1200 Building Program.)

- Business services are the number one industry in terms of number of employees and establishments, followed by finance, insurance and the retail trade (C40, 2013).

- Melbourne emits some 5,994 kilotons of CO_2 equivalent per year, 74% of which comes from industry and commercial buildings (as of 2012). Commercial buildings alone generate more than half of the city's GHG emissions (C40, 2013). Therefore, improvements in the commercial building sector are key.

- The city has set the target of reducing carbon emissions from the commercial sector by 25% and from the residential sector by 20% (C40, 2013).

Actions

- As part of the most ambitious goal of becoming carbon-neutral by 2020, in March 2010 the City of Melbourne launched the 1200 Buildings Program.

- The 1200 Buildings Program aims to encourage and support building owners and managers to improve commercial buildings' energy and water efficiency and reduce the amount of waste going from these buildings to landfills. In particular, it has set the goal of encouraging the environmental retrofitting of around two-thirds of the municipality's commercial stock, which are responsible for nearly half of Melbourne's CO_2 emissions, within 10 to 15 years (C40, 2013; City of Melbourne, 2014; NYC Global Partners, 2011a).

- By improving energy efficiency by around 38%, the commercial building sector alone could eliminate 383,000 tons of GHG emissions every year (City of Melbourne, 2014).

- Managing water is also a priority for the administration and the city has a target of reducing potable water use in the commercial sector by 5 billion liters (City of Melbourne, 2015a).

Sources of CO_2 (eq.) emissions

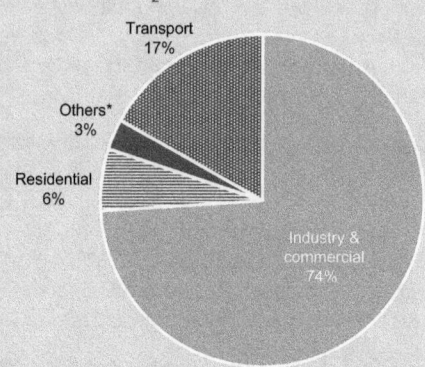

* Others includes emissions from water and waste.

Source: Prepared by the authors based on C40, 2013.

- This program was the first of its kind in Australia. The Sustainable Buildings Program integrates many strategies and initiatives and includes both "obligations" and "rewards" for building owners and managers. On the one hand, it sets minimum environmental requirements for new buildings through its energy and water policy. On the other hand, it provides tailored support to building owners and offers financial incentives through the environmental upgrade agreements, allowing building owners to overcome financial difficulties and giving owners support to retrofit existing buildings (the City Switch and Smart Blocks programs) (C40, 2013; Cleary and Cotter, 2012). The Sustainable Buildings Program is voluntary but offers significant incentives to retrofit.

- The projects include the installation of a trigeneration system, high-efficiency chillers, cooling towers, lighting system upgrades, and heating and air conditioning units and controls (C40, 2012).

- Melbourne Council invested A$1 million in the 1200 Buildings Program in the 2009–10 financial year and another A$1 million in 2010–11. Financial support was also received from the state and national governments. Victoria's state government provided A$500,000 to support the financial mechanism, and the Australian government an additional A$200,000 for a cost-benefit analysis toolkit (Cleary and Cotter, 2012). Melbourne City Council also made a commitment to invest more in the following years.

Outcomes

- The program has benefited building owners and managers by reducing energy costs and the use of water and it has benefited the whole of society by cutting GHG emissions and air pollution.

Retrofit activity in Melbourne

Source: City of Melbourne.

- Political support and leadership have been crucial in the process, as has the involvement of different stakeholders, such as building owners, the state government and technical experts, through the development of the program.

- The 1200 Building Program is still in place (it is a 10-year plan) and it has the potential to develop approximately A$2 billion worth of investment and create around 8,000 green jobs (City of Melbourne, 2015a).

- As of 2013, the 1200 Buildings Program had supported 10% of the building sector to retrofit and there were 56 public signatories (representing 5% of all the buildings), including large commercial groups: GPT Group, ING, Stockland, and Asia Pacific Group (C40, 2013; RE-GREEN, 2013). Each signatory has pledged to undertake an environmental retrofit by 2020 (NYC Global Partners, 2011a)

- Those in charge of a further 150 buildings are considering or in the process of retrofitting (C40, 2015).

- The environmental upgrade agreement initiative has proved to be an innovative and successful mechanism to finance projects (Cleary and Cotter, 2012). As of 2013, four buildings had used such agreements to access finance to retrofit, representing A$5.6 million of investment, with the aim of saving 5,660 tons in carbon emissions and A$491,000 in energy costs per year (C40, 2013). Fifty additional buildings had expressed an interest in signing up for the agreements.

- The project also aims to reduce the annual use of potable water in the commercial sector by 5 gigaliters, an important step in a water-scarce city at risk from the effects of climate change (C40, 2015).

- Melbourne was ranked the world's most livable city by the Economist Intelligence Unit in 2011, 2012 and 2013.

- The 1200 Buildings Program has received two prestigious awards: in 2013, its Sustainable Buildings Program was the winner in the efficient built environment category of the C40 and Siemens Climate Leadership Awards; and it won the United Nations Association of Australia World Environment Day Sustainability Award (C40, 2013; RE-GREEN, 2013).

***

c. Public Lighting

Lighting is a large and rapidly growing source of energy demand and GHG emissions. The world's total electricity consumption for lighting in 2005 represented almost 20% of total electricity consumption (IEA, 2006a). Commercial and residential buildings, as well as industry, are responsible for most of the consumption but public or outdoor lighting consumes a small proportion.

Increasing urbanization will lead to a rise in demand for public lighting. In order to improve the energy efficiency of public lighting as well as energy use and consumption, many cities are implementing diverse initiatives using so-called intelligent streetlights. These lighting systems save energy by using sensors on streetlights that allow lights to turn on and off automatically when people walk by them at night. Amsterdam and Glasgow are two cities testing a pilot of these systems.[6] Another strategy that some cities are implementing is the use of more efficient streetlights, such as LEDs. (See the panel Best Practice: Los Angeles below.)

---

[6] For more information on these two streetlight pilot programs see: "Flexible Street Lighting" (http://amsterdamsmartcity.com/projects/detail/id/62/slug/flexible-street-lighting?lang=en) and "Intelligent Street Lighting" (http://futurecity.glasgow.gov.uk/intelligent-street-lighting).

Policies, legislation and regulations

New applied technologies and innovations

BEST PRACTICE: LOS ANGELES
– LED street lighting retrofit

Los Angeles (L.A.) is the most populous city in California and the second largest city in the United States after New York. It has a population of 3.9 million in an area of 1,302 km². The L.A.-Long Beach-Santa Ana metropolitan area has around 13 million inhabitants. The metropolitan area has a per capita income of more than $50,000 and its GDP is more than $700 billion (ESMAP, 2011). Moreover, L.A. is a center of new ideas and a cluster for different industries such as entertainment, aerospace, fashion, biomedicine, among many others.

The city of Los Angeles at night

Source: Pixabay, CC0.

Context

- In May 2007, Mayor Antonio R. Villaraigosa unveiled Green L.A.: An Action Plan to Lead the Nation in Fighting Global Warming, with the aim of making the city a world leader in the fight against climate change (ESMAP, 2011).

- One of the areas with huge potential for energy efficiency and energy savings was L.A.'s public lighting system. Energy costs were a growing concern for the city administration.

- The Los Angeles street lighting system is the second largest in the United States, with more than 200,000 street lights that used almost 200,000 MWh per year, providing illumination for vehicular and pedestrian traffic (ESMAP, 2011; NYC Global Partners, 2011b).

Actions

- In 2009 the city launched the Light Emitting Diode (LED) Streetlight Replacement Program, with the aim of replacing 140,000 streetlights with LED units over a five-year period (2009–14).

- The LED technology provided a significant reduction in energy consumption.

- The project was the largest LED street lighting retrofit ever undertaken (ESMAP, 2011).

- The program, implemented by the Los Angeles Bureau of Street Lighting, had the goal of achieving 40% energy savings in street lighting, reducing carbon emissions and light pollution, improving safety, and enhancing the quality of municipal street lighting.

- The estimated total cost of the project was $57 million, funded through a loan and the Street Lighting Maintenance Assessment Fund (NYC Global Partners, 2011b).

Outcomes

- The program has successfully replaced more than 140,000 existing streetlight fixtures in the city with LED units.

- The expected energy savings were exceeded. Electricity costs were cut by 63% and carbon emissions by 47,583 tons a year (City of Los Angeles, 2015).

- These savings will pay back the money borrowed and provide energy and maintenance savings in the coming years.

- Night crime fell between 2009 and 2011 (City of Los Angeles, 2015).

- Price is key when retrofitting lighting in a city. The price of the LED lights fell significantly during the program, from $432 each in 2009 to $245 in 2012, and the price continues to decrease (City of Los Angeles, 2015). However, it might still be too high for small or low-income cities.

- This is a good example of how green technology can be both environmentally responsible and cost-effective. It also shows how municipalities can use their unique positions to initiate change in favor of new types of energy and environmental technology.

**

4. Concluding Remarks

As seen in this volume, our planet is already straining from the impact of human activities and rapid urbanization on the environment. Most of these environmental challenges need a global approach to be tackled. The Paris Agreement reached in December 2015 at the COP21 Climate Change Conference is a first step in this regard. At the COP21 Conference, almost 200 countries agreed to attempt to limit the rise in global temperatures to well below 2°C above preindustrial levels by the end of the century – among other commitments such as countries making stronger pledges to cut carbon emissions every five years and rich countries helping poorer nations by providing finance to adapt to climate change (UNFCCC, 2015).

COP21 represented the first recognition that global action was needed to reduce the risks and impact of climate change significantly. However, as some of the best practices highlighted in this volume suggest, policy strength at the city level has also proven to be very effective in diminishing the negative consequences of urbanization processes on the environment. Local administrations can undertake concrete actions to reduce GHG emissions, improve energy efficiency and promote more environmentally friendly urban development patterns.

This volume has shown that cities around the world can become hubs of innovation and implement groundbreaking strategies to reduce the negative effects of urbanization. The book has explored some of the current initiatives and best practices that different cities have implemented to promote sustainable and resilient paths of urban development. The involvement of all key stakeholders and civil society at local levels is needed to come up with the right strategies for each local context. Effective policies can differ between more mature cities and emerging and developing cities or between compact cities and sprawling cities. Therefore, each city needs to start from its existing strengths and concrete challenges and build upon them.

The most strategic environmental urban solutions are those that harmonize the opportunities and challenges of rapid urbanization. City managers need to take a holistic approach to environmental problems since actions in one area can also lead to progress in other areas. For instance, improving aspects such as transport and urban planning can result in better air quality and/or more efficient waste management and sanitation. Therefore, the environment is not only a key dimension in the future design and management of cities but is also very much related to other critical dimensions of cities – such as mobility, the economy, urban planning, technology, human capital and governance.

Cities must therefore become more compact, denser and better-managed, with connected infrastructure and coordinated governance in order to move to more environmentally sustainable patterns of growth. As shown through this book, many actions at different levels have already been designed to solve the environmental challenges of cities, and substantial progress has been made in this regard. However, much more can still be done and improved in order to achieve more sustainable and livelier cities for all.

5. References

Abarca Guerrero, L., Maas, G., and Hogland, W. (2013). "Solid Waste Management Challenges for Cities in Developing Countries." *Waste Management* 33(1), 220–232.

Baldé, C.P., Wang, F., Kuehr, R., and Huisman, J. (2015). *The Global E-Waste Monitor – 2014*. Bonn: United Nations University, IAS – SCYCLE (Sustainable Cycles).

Barcelona Activa (2014). *Barcelona Data Sheet 2014*, from http://www.slideshare.net/barcelonactiva/barcelona-datasheet-eng.

Berrone, P., Ricart, J.E., and Blázquez, M.L. (2014). "Vancouver: The Challenge of Becoming the Greenest City." IESE case study SM-1612.

Blake, A. (n.d.). *Pocket Parks*, from http://depts.washington.edu/open2100/pdf/2_OpenSpaceTypes/Open_Space_Types/pocket_parks.pdf.

Build Green (2011). "Definition: What Is a Green Building?" from http://buildgreen.co.nz/definition.html.

Burke, J. (2015). "Child Health Fears at the Most Polluted Spot in the World's Most Polluted City." *The Guardian*, June 24. Retrieved from http://www.theguardian.com/environment/2015/jun/24/indian-children-fall-victim-to-delhis-appalling-pollution.

C40 (2012). "Case Study: 1200 Buildings Program" from http://www.c40.org/case_studies/1200-buildings-program.

C40 (2013). *City Climate Leadership Awards: Melbourne Climate Close-Up*, from http://www.c40.org/2013-close-up/melbourne-closeup.pdf.

Caamaño-Martín, E. (2008). "Strategies for the Development of PV in Barcelona." PV UPSCALE.

Carle, J. (2015). "Climate Change Seen as Top Global Threat." Spring 2015 Pew Research Center Global Attitudes Survey. Retrieved from www.pewglobal.org/2015/07/14/climate-change-seen-as-top-global-threat.

City of Copenhagen (2012). CPH 2025 Climate Plan: A Green, Smart and Carbon Neutral City. Copenhagen: Technical and Environmental Administration, City of Copenhagen. Retrieved from http://kk.sites.itera.dk/apps/kk_pub2/pdf/983_jkP0ekKMyD.pdf.

City of Los Angeles (2015). "Bureau of Street Lighting," from http://bsl.lacity.org/led.html.

City of Melbourne (2014). "1200 Buildings Advice Sheet."

City of Melbourne (2015a). "1200 Buildings," from http://www.melbourne.vic.gov.au/1200buildings/Pages/About1200Buildings.aspx.

City of Melbourne (2015b). City of Melbourne - Daily population Estimates and Forecasts. 2015 Updates, from http://www.melbourne.vic.gov.au/SiteCollectionDocuments/daily-population-estimates-and-forecasts-report-2015.pdf.

City of Vancouver (2012). Greenest City: 2020 Action Plan. Retrived from http://vancouver.ca/files/cov/Greenest-city-action-plan.pdf.

City of Vancouver (2015). Greenest City Action Plan: Past, Present, and Future. Retrieved from http://vancouver.ca/files/cov/greenest-city-action-plan-update-presentation-06-23-2015.pdf.

Cleary, H., and Cotter, B. (2012). City of Melbourne, Australia: Building an Eco-City, Building a Sustainable City. Melbourne: ICLEI.

CNN (2015). "Why Is This City the Worst Air Polluter?" April 14. Retrieved from http://edition.cnn.com/2015/04/13/asia/sumnima-udas-new-delhi-air-quality/index.html.

Creutzig, F., Baiocchi, G., Bierkandt, R., Pichler, P.-P., and Seto, K.C. (2014). "Global Typology of Urban Energy Use and Potentials for an Urbanization Mitigation Wedge." Proceedings of the National Academy of Science 112(20), 6283–6288.

De Sherbinin, A., Schiller, A., and Pulsipher, A. (2007). "The vulnerability of global cities to climate hazards." Environment and Urbanization, 19(1), 39-64.

Dimitriadi, D. (2013). "Lack of Green Spaces? Pocket Parks Are the Solution," March 22. Retrieved from http://www.globalsiteplans.com/environmental-design/lack-of-green-spaces-pocket-parks-are-the-solution.

Endesa (2014). Smartcity Malaga: A Model of Sustainable Energy Management for Cities of the Future.

Enerdata (2013). *The State of Global Energy Efficiency: Global and Sectorial Energy Efficiency Trends*. Zurich: ABB Ltd.

EPA (United States Environmental Protection Agency) (2013). "Green Building," from http://www.epa.gov/greenbuilding/pubs/about.htm.

ESMAP (Energy Sector Management Assistance Program) (2011). "Good Practices in City Energy Efficiency: Los Angeles, USA – Light Emitting Diode (LED) Street Lighting Retrofit."

Euricur, PWC, and IHS (2014). *Innovative City Strategies for Delivering Sustainable Competitiveness*.

Fang, W. (2014). "How Cities Can Save Trillions, Curb Climate Change, and Improve Public Health." Retrieved from the World Resources Institute website at http://www.wri.org/blog/2014/09/how-cities-can-save-trillions-curb-climate-change-and-improve-public-health.

Floater, G., and Rode, P. (2014). *Cities and the New Climate Economy: The Transformative Role of Global Urban Growth*. New Climate Economy Cities Paper 01, London: LSE Cities, London School of Economics and Political Science.

Floater, G., Rode, P., and Zenghelis, D. (2013). *Stockholm: Green Economy Leader Report*, report by the Economics of Green Cities Programme. London: LSE Cities, London School of Economics and Political Science.

Floater, G., Rode, P., and Zenghelis, D. (2014). *Copenhagen: Green Economy Leader Report*, report by the Economics of Green Cities Programme. London: LSE Cities, London School of Economics and Political Science.

Gairola, S., and Noresah, M.S. (2010). "Emerging Trend of Urban Green Space Research and the Implications for Safeguarding Biodiversity: A Viewpoint." *Nature and Science* 8(7).

Gerdes, J. (2013). "Copenhagen's Ambitious Push to be Carbon-Neutral by 2025." *The Guardian*, April 12. Retrieved from http://www.theguardian.com/environment/2013/apr/12/copenhagen-push-carbon-neutral-2025.

GeSI and BCG (2012). *GeSI SMARTer 2020: The Role of ICT in Driving a Sustainable Future*. Global eSustainability Initiative and The Boston Consulting Group.

Global City Indicators Facility (2014). "Melbourne," from http://www.cityindicators.org/ParticipantsInfo.aspx?cID=419.

Guevara-Stone, L. (2014). "Barcelona: Spain's City of the Sun." RenewEconomy, August 12. Retrieved from http://reneweconomy.com.au/2014/barcelona-spains-city-of-the-sun-54062.

Hoornweg, D., and Bhada-Tata, P. (2012). *What a Waste : A Global Review of Solid Waste Management*. Washington, D.C.: World Bank.

Hoornweg, D., Bhada-Tata, P., and Kennedy, C. (2013). "Environment: Waste Production Must Peak This Century." *Nature* 502(7473). Retrieved from http://www.nature.com/news/environment-waste-production-must-peak-this-century-1.14032.

Hower, M. (2015). "Grid or No Grid, Efficiency is Key to Powering the Global South." GreenBiz, September 18. Retrieved from http://www.greenbiz.com/article/grid-or-no-grid-efficiency-key-powering-global-south?utm_medium=e-mail&utm_source=e-news&utm_campaign=verge&mkt_tok=3RkMMJWWfF-9wsRouuqXJZKXonjHpfsX56%2B4vWaG%2FIMI%2F0ER3fOvrPUfGjI4JT-8JiI%2BSLDwEYGJlv6SgFSLHEMa5qw7gMXRQ%3D.

Idescat (Statistical Institute of Catalonia) (2015). "The Municipality in Figures: Barcelona," from http://www.idescat.cat/emex/?id=080193&lang=en.

IEA (2006a). *Light's Labour's Lost: Policies for Energy-Efficient Lighting*. Paris: International Energy Agency (IEA).

IEA (2006b). *World Energy Outlook 2006*. Paris: International Energy Agency (IEA).

IEA (2014a). "Energy Efficiency: A Key Tool for Boosting Economic and Social Development," September 9. Retrieved from http://www.iea.org/newsroomandevents/pressreleases/2014/september/energy-efficiency-a-key-tool-for-boosting-economic-and-social-development.html.

IEA (2014b). "Global Energy Efficiency Market 'an Invisible Powerhouse' Worth at Least USD 310 Billion Per Year," October 8. Retrieved from http://www.iea.org/newsroomandevents/pressreleases/2014/october/global-energy-efficiency-market-an-invisible-powerhouse-at-least-usd-310byr.html.

IEA (2014c). *World Energy Outlook 2014*. Paris: International Energy Agency (IEA).

IPCC (Intergovernmental Panel on Climate Change) (2014). *Climate Change 2014: Mitigation of Climate Change*. Cambridge, United Kingdom, and New York, United States: Cambridge University Press.

IUCN (International Union for Conservation of Nature) (2014). "Environmental Governance," from http://www.iucn.org/about/work/programmes/environmental_law/elp_work/elp_work_issues/elp_work_governance/.

Mao, Y. (2014). *Clean Technology Sector: Singapore*. Brussels: Belgian Foreign Trade Agency.

Marques, A., and Pujol, T. (2014). "Barcelona, Spain: Using Solar Energy – Supporting Community Energy Self-Sufficiency." *ICLEI Case Studies* 173. Barcelona: ICLEI.

Mooney, C. (2015). "To Truly Grasp What We're Doing to the Planet, You Need to Understand This Gigantic Measurement." *The Washington Post*, July 1. Retrieved from http://www.washingtonpost.com/news/energy-environment/wp/2015/07/01/meet-the-gigaton-the-huge-unit-that-scientists-use-to-track-planetary-change/.

Mutizwa-Mangiza, N.D., Arimah, B.C., Jensen, I., Yemeru, E.A., and Kinyanjui., M.K. (2011). *Global Report on Human Settlements 2011: Cities and Climate Change*. London and Washington, D.C.: United Nations Human Settlements Programme (UNHabitat).

Nanyang Technological University (2014). "Singapore's Water Solution," Water Conservation in Singapore blog, from https://blogs.ntu.edu.sg/hp331-2014-51/?page_id=25.

New Climate Economy (2014). *Better Growth, Better Climate: The New Climate Economy Report*. Washington, D.C.: Global Commission on the Economy and Climate.

New Climate Economy (2015). *Seizing the Global Opportunity: Partnerships for Better Growth and Better Climate*. Washington, D.C.: Global Commission on the Economy and Climate.

NYC Global Partners (2011a). "Best Practice: Green Buildings Retrofit Program."

NYC Global Partners (2011b). "Best Practice: LED Street Lighting System."

NYC Global Partners (2011c). "Best Practice: Promoting Solar Energy."

OECD (Organisation for Economic Cooperation and Development) (2012). Environmental Outlook to 2050: The Consequences of Inaction. Paris: OECD.

Oliveira de Medeiros, L. (2012). "Belo Horizonte, Brazil – Waste to Energy for More Effective Landfill Site Management." *ICLEI Case Studies*.

Olivier, J.G.J., Janssens-Maenhout, G., Muntean, M., and Peters, J.A.H.W. (2014). *Trends in Global CO_2 Emissions: 2014 Report*. The Hague: PBL Netherlands Environmental Assessment Agency. Institute for Environment and Sustainability (IES) of the European Commission's Joint Research Centre (JRC).

Prüss-Üstün, A., and Corvalán, C. (2006). *Preventing Disease Through Healthy Environments: Towards an Estimate of the Environmental Burden of Disease*. Geneva: World Health Organization (WHO).

PUB (Public Utilities Board) (2014). "Ensuring Water Sustainability," from http://www.pub.gov.sg.

RE-GREEN (2013). "Case of the Month – Melbourne," from http://www.re-green.eu/en/go/case-of-the-month---melbourne.

Rode, P., and Burdett, R. (2011). *Cities: Investing in Energy and Resource Efficiency*. Nairobi: United Nations Environment Programme (UNEP).

Rode, P., and Floater, G. (2013). *Going Green: How Cities Are Leading the Next Economy*. London: LSE Cities, ICLEI and the Global Green Growth Institute.

Rust, E. (2014). "Map Some Noise: How Your Smartphone Can Help Tackle City Sound Pollution." *The Guardian*, September 12. Retrieved from http://www.theguardian.com/cities/2014/sep/12/map-noise-how-smartphone-help-tackle-city-sound-pollution-noisetube.

Saunders, T., and Baeck, P. (2015). *Rethinking Smart Cities From the Ground Up*. London: Nesta.

Schwarz, V. (2010). *Promoting Energy Efficiency in Buildings: Lessons Learned From International Experience*. New York: United Nations Development Programme (UNDP).

Seto K.C., Dhakal, S., Bigio, A., Blanco, H., Delgado, G.C., Dewar, D., Huang, L., Inaba, A., Kansal, A., Lwasa, S., McMahon, J.E., Müller, D.B., Murakami, J., Nagendra, H., and Ramaswami, A. (2014). "Human Settlements, Infrastructure and Spatial Planning." In Edenhoder, O., et al., *Climate Change 2014: Mitigation of Climate Change. Contribution of Working Group III to the Fifth Assessment Report of the Intergovernmental Panel on Climate Change*. Cambridge, United Kingdom and New York, N.Y., USA: Cambridge University Press.

SF Environment (San Francisco Department of the Environment) (2015). "Zero Waste - Goals" from http://www.sfenvironment.org/zero-waste.

Sustainable Urban Futures (2015). "Cities and Climate Change," from http://urban.ias.unu.edu/index.php/cities-and-climate-change.

Thiagarajan, K. (2015). "Pollution-Proofing Tips." The Swaddle. Retrieved from http://theswaddle.com/air-pollution-proof-your-health.

UN (United Nations) (2014). "'Water for Life' UN-Water Best Practices Award – 2014 edition: Winners," from http://www.un.org/waterforlifedecade/winners2014.shtml.

UNEP (United Nations Environment Programme) (2011). *Call to Action*, from http://www.unep.org/sbci/pdfs/Cop17/SBCI_Call_to_Action_November_2011_web.pdf.

UNFCCC (United Nations Framework Convention on Climate Change) (2015). *Adoption of the Paris Agreement*, FCCC/CP/2015/L.9. Paris: Conference of the Parties.

UN-Habitat (2008a). "Cities and Climate Change," part 3.2 in López Moreno, E., et al., *State of the World's Cities 2008/2009*. Nairobi: United Nations Human Settlements Programme (UNHabitat).

UN-Habitat (2008b). "Energy Consumption in Cities," part 3.4 in López Moreno, E., et al., *State of the World's Cities 2008/2009*. Nairobi: United Nations Human Settlements Programme (UNHabitat).

UN-Habitat (2010). *Solid Waste Management in the World's Cities: Water and Sanitation in the World's Cities 2010*. Nairobi: United Nations Human Settlements Programme (UNHabitat).

UNHabitat (2012a). "Urban Themes: Climate Change," from http://unhabitat.org/urban-themes/climate-change.

UN-Habitat (2012b). "Urban Themes: Energy," from http://unhabitat.org/urban-themes/energy.

UN-Habitat (2012c). "Urban Themes: Water & Sanitation," from http://unhabitat.org/urban-themes/water-and-sanitation-2.

UN-Habitat, CBD (Convention on Biological Diversity) and UN-Women (2016). *Habitat III Issue Paper: 11 – Public Space*. Paper to be presented at the United Nations Conference on Housing and Sustainable Urban Development, Quito.

Vander Veen, C. (2015). "Smart Cities Start with Behavior Change." FutureStructure, from http://www.govtech.com/fs/Smart-Cities-Start-with-Behavior-Change.html.

Vázquez, M. (2011). "How Much Green Space Does Your City Have?" Sustainable Cities International blog, July 13. Retrieved from https://plusnetwork.wordpress.com/2011/07/13/how-many-metres-of-green-space-does-your-city-have.

WHO (2011). *Burden of Disease From Environmental Noise*. Bonn: WHO European Centre for Environment and Health.

WHO (2014a). "7 Million Premature Deaths Annually Linked to Air Pollution." March 25. Retrieved from http://www.who.int/mediacentre/news/releases/2014/air-pollution/en.

WHO (2014b). "Air Quality Deteriorating in Many of the World's Cities." May 7. Retrieved from http://www.who.int/mediacentre/news/releases/2014/air-quality/en.

WHO (2014c). WHO's Ambient Air Pollution database - Update 2014.

WHO and UNICEF (2010). *Progress on Sanitation and Drinking-Water: 2010 Update*. Geneva and New York: WHO and UNICEF.

WHO and UNICEF (2014). *Progress on Drinking Water and Sanitation: 2014 Update*. Geneva and New York: WHO and UNICEF.

World Bank (2012). "'What a Waste' Report Shows Alarming Rise in Amount, Costs of Garbage." June 6. Retrieved from http://www.worldbank.org/en/news/feature/2012/06/06/report-shows-alarming-rise-in-amount-costs-of-garbage.

World Bank (2013). "Global Waste on Pace to Triple by 2100." October 30. Retrieved from http://www.worldbank.org/en/news/feature/2013/10/30/global-waste-on-pace-to-triple.

World Bank (2014). "World Development Indicators: Freshwater," from http://wdi.worldbank.org/table/3.5.

World Bank and ClimateWorks Foundation (2014). *Climate-Smart Development: Adding Up the Benefits of Actions That Help Build Prosperity, End Poverty and Combat Climate Change*. Washington, D.C., and San Francisco: World Bank and ClimateWorks Foundation.

World Resources Institute (2015). CAIT Climate Data Explorer.

WWF Global (2015). "Ecological Footprint," from http://wwf.panda.org/about_our_earth/teacher_resources/webfieldtrips/ecological_balance/eco_footprint.

6. Appendix I: Additional Resources

On the IESE Cities in Motion Strategies website you will find additional related material and resources. Check the following link regularly to access our latest publications:

• IESE Cities in Motion Strategies: http://www.iese.edu/cim.

Additionally, the authors recommend the following Internet resources for more information on the topic:

• C40 Cities: http://www.c40.org.

• Cities Alliance: http://www.citiesalliance.org.

• Energy Cities: http://www.energy-cities.eu.

• Eurocities: http://www.eurocities.eu.

• European Environment Agency (EEA): http://www.eea.europa.eu.

• Global Footprint Network: http://www.footprintnetwork.org.

• Global Green Growth Institute: http://gggi.org.

• Green City Index: http://www.siemens.com/entry/cc/en/greencityindex.htm.

• GrowSmarter: http://www.grow-smarter.eu/home.

• ICLEI – Local Governments for Sustainability: http://www.iclei.org.

• Intergovernmental Panel on Climate Change (IPCC): http://www.ipcc.ch.

• International Energy Agency (IEA): http://www.iea.org.

• International Institute for Environment and Development: http://www.iied.org.

• Sustainable Cities International (SCI): http://www.sustainablecities.net/our-info.

- UN-Habitat: http://unhabitat.org.
- U.S. Energy Information Administration (EIA): http://www.eia.gov.
- World Bank: http://www.worldbank.org.
- World Health Organization (WHO): http://www.who.int.
- World Resources Institute (WRI): http://www.wri.org.

7. Appendix II: Cities in Motion Index – Environmental Dimension

This appendix includes a brief presentation of the IESE Cities in Motion Index, focusing on the environmental dimension. For more information on the index, please check the IESE Cities in Motion website www.iese.edu/cim, with all our latest publications.

CITIES IN MOTION INDEX

The Cities in Motion Index (**CIMI**) has been designed with the aim of constructing a "breakthrough" indicator in terms of its completeness, characteristics, comparability and the quality and objectivity of its information. Its goal is to enable measurement of the future sustainability of the world's main cities as well as the quality of life of their inhabitants.

The **CIMI** aims to help the public and governments to understand the performance of 10 fundamental dimensions for a city: governance, urban planning, public management, technology, the environment, international outreach, social cohesion, mobility and transportation, human capital, and the economy. Thanks to its broad and integrated vision of the city, the Cities in Motion Index enables to recognize the strengths and weaknesses of each city, allowing to identify effective solutions.

The 2016 edition is the third consecutive **CIMI**, covering the years 2013, 2014 and 2015. It includes a total of 181 cities, of which 72 are capitals representing 60 different countries, as well as 77 indicators measuring the 10 relevant dimensions.

RANKING *CIMI* 2015

New York City (United States) is in first place in the overall ranking, driven by its performance in the dimensions of the economy (first place), technology (third place) and in human capital, public management, governance, international outreach, and mobility and transportation (fourth place). However, for another year, it continues to be in very low positions in the dimensions of social cohesion (position 161) and in environment (position 93). Following New York, we find London (UK) in the second place of the ranking and Paris (France) in the third place.

Of the 10 top positions of the ranking, four cities are in the U.S. (New York, San Francisco, Boston and Chicago); four cities are in Europe (London, Paris, Amsterdam and Geneva); one is in Asia (Seoul) and one in Oceania (Sydney).

TABLE A1. CITY RANKING. TOP 10

CIMI 2015	City (Country)
1	New York City (United States)
2	London (United Kingdom)
3	Paris (France)
4	San Francisco (United States)
5	Boston (United States)
6	Amsterdam (Netherlands)
7	Chicago (United States)
8	Seoul (South Korea)
9	Geneva (Switzerland)
10	Sydney (Australia)

ENVIRONMENTAL DIMENSION

Sustainable development of a city can be defined as development "that meets the needs of the present without compromising the ability of future generations to meet their own needs".[1] In this respect, factors such as improving environmental sustainability through antipollution plans, support for green buildings and alternative energy, efficient water management, and policies that help counter the effects of climate change are essential for the long-term sustainability of cities.

Since the **CIMI** also seeks to measure the environmental sustainability of cities, the environment is included as one of the essential aspects of measurement. Table A2 sets out the indicators selected in this dimension, with their description and source.

TABLE A2. ENVIRONMENTAL INDICATORS

Indicator	Description / Unit of measurement	Source
CO_2 emissions	Carbon dioxide emissions that come from the burning of fossil fuels and the manufacture of cement. Measured in kilotons (kt).	World Bank
CO_2 emission index	CO_2 emission index	Numbeo
Methane emissions	Methane emissions that arise from human activities such as agriculture and the industrial production of methane. Measured in kt of CO_2 equivalent	World Bank
Percentage of the population with access to the water supply	Percentage of the population with reasonable access to an appropriate quantity of water resulting from an improvement in the water supply	World Bank

---

[1] Definition used in 1987 by the UN's World Commission on Environment and Development, created in 1983.

PM2.5	PM2.5 measures the amount of particles in the air whose diameter is less than 2.5 μm. Annual mean	World Health Organization
PM10	PM10 measures the amount of particles in the air whose diameter is less than 10 μm. Annual mean	World Health Organization
Pollution index	Pollution index	Numbeo
Environmental performance index	Environmental performance index (from 1 = poor to 100 = good)	Yale University

The indicators selected include measurements of air pollution sources and water quality in cities, which are indicators of the quality of life of their inhabitants, as well as the sustainability of their production or urban matrix.

Carbon dioxide emissions come from the burning of fossil fuels and the manufacture of cement, while methane emissions arise from human activities such as agriculture and the industrial production of methane. CO_2 and methane emissions are the main measures that are commonly used to quantify the degree of air pollution, since they are highly correlated with global warming and climate change. In fact, the decline in these indicators' values is included as a target in the Kyoto Protocol.

Other very important indicators for air pollution in cities are $PM_{2.5}$ and PM_{10}, a designation that corresponds to small particles, solid or liquid, of dust, ash, soot, metal particles, cement or pollen, scattered in the atmosphere and whose diameter is less than 2.5 and 10 micrometers (μm) respectively. These particles are formed, primarily by inorganic compounds such as silicates and aluminates, heavy metals and organic material associated with carbon particles (soot). These indicators are commonly used in the indices that seek to measure the state of environmental pollution. These indicators are complemented by the information provided by the city pollution index, which estimates the overall pollution in the city. The greatest weight is given to those cities with the highest air pollution.

Finally, the Environmental Performance Index (EPI), calculated by Yale University, is an indicator based on the measurement of two large dimensions related to the environment: environmental health and ecosystem vitality. The first is divided into three subdimensions: effects on human health of air pollution, effects of water quality on human health, and environmental burden of diseases. Ecosystem vitality contains seven subdimensions: effects on the ecosystem of air pollution, effects on the ecosystem of water quality, biodiversity and habitat, afforestation, fish, and climate change. Given the completeness of this indicator – which covers almost all aspects related to measuring the state and evolution of the environment in a city, complemented by the other indicators that the *CIMI* incorporates – it is considered that the environmental dimension is represented proportionately.

The indicators of PM_{10}, $PM_{2.5}$, CO_2 emissions, methane emissions, and the rate of pollution bear a negative sign in the dimension's indicator, while the remaining indicators have a positive effect on the environment.

RANKING - ENVIRONMENTAL DIMENSION

In the environmental dimension, the cities that are best positioned are Zurich (Switzerland) and Helsinki (Finland). These cities are in the top of the Environmental Performance Index (EPI) and have low levels of pollution and CO_2 emissions. All cities in the top 10 for this dimension are European.

TABLE A3. RANKING BY DIMENSION: THE ENVIRONMENT

City	Environment Ranking	CIMI 2015 Ranking
Zurich, Switzerland	1	14
Helsinki, Finland	2	25
Munich, Germany	3	21
Tallinn, Estonia	4	54
Vienna, Austria	5	26
Basel, Switzerland	6	42
Linz, Austria	7	63
Stockholm, Sweden	8	27
Geneva, Switzerland	9	9
Oslo, Norway	10	28
Frankfurt, Germany	11	35
Prague, Czech Republic	12	45
Hamburg, Germany	13	41
Berlin, Germany	14	16
Copenhagen, Denmark	15	11
Stuttgart, Germany	16	51
Goteborg, Sweden	17	57
Bratislava, Slovakia	18	83
Auckland, New Zealand	19	29
London, United Kingdom	20	2
Valencia, Spain	21	49
Dublin, Ireland	22	36
A Coruna, Spain	23	60
Singapore, Singapore	24	22
Duisburg, Germany	25	73
Seville, Spain	26	67
Tokyo, Japan	27	12
Ljubljana, Slovenia	28	86

City	Environment Ranking	CIMI 2015 Ranking
Melbourne, Australia	29	17
London, Canada	30	37
Ottawa, Canada	31	30
Sydney, Australia	32	10
Lisbon, Portugal	33	62
Naples, Italy	34	90
Liverpool, United Kingdom	35	48
Vilnius, Lithuania	36	89
Leeds, United Kingdom	37	71
Birmingham, United Kingdom	38	47
Porto, Portugal	39	76
Nottingham, United Kingdom	40	75
Vancouver, Canada	41	20
Amsterdam, Netherlands	42	6
Kuwait, Kuwait	43	119
Riga, Latvia	44	78
Nagoya, Japan	45	87
Florence, Italy	46	50
Budapest, Hungary	47	68
Cologne, Germany	48	52
Bilbao, Spain	49	69
Rotterdam, Netherlands	50	70
Eindhoven, Netherlands	51	59
Glasgow, United Kingdom	52	46
Seoul, South Korea	53	8
Madrid, Spain	54	34
Malaga, Spain	55	58
Nice, France	56	61
Montreal, Canada	57	38

City	Environment Ranking	CIMI 2015 Ranking
Lyon, France	58	55
Manchester, United Kingdom	59	43
Antwerp, Belgium	60	77
Marseille, France	61	72
Hong Kong, China	62	39
Osaka, Japan	63	56
Paris, France	64	3
Barcelona, Spain	65	33
Warsaw, Poland	66	74
Zagreb, Croatia	67	107
Milan, Italy	68	44
Brussels, Belgium	69	32
Lille, France	70	79
Wroclaw, Poland	71	94
Belgrade, Serbia	72	114
Athens, Greece	73	113
Haifa, Israel	74	101
Sofia, Bulgaria	75	95
Rome, Italy	76	81
Almaty, Kazakhstan	77	125
Minsk, Belarus	78	137
Tel Aviv, Israel	79	97
Jerusalem, Israel	80	105
Toronto, Canada	81	24
Turin, Italy	82	82
Daejeon, South Korea	83	96
San Jose, Costa Rica	84	131
Busan, South Korea	85	91
Daegu, South Korea	86	98

City	Environment Ranking	CIMI 2015 Ranking
Bursa, Turkey	87	128
Boston, United States	88	5
Chicago, United States	89	7
Montevideo, Uruguay	90	121
Santiago, Chile	91	80
San Francisco, United States	92	4
New York City, United States	93	1
Medellin, Colombia	94	99
Tbilisi, Georgia	95	135
Brasilia, Brazil	96	136
Baltimore, United States	97	18
Washington, D.C., United States	98	13
Quito, Ecuador	99	132
Porto Alegre, Brazil	100	118
Jidda, Saudi Arabia	101	115
Cordoba, Argentina	102	106
Kuala Lumpur, Malaysia	103	88
Rosario, Argentina	104	134
Ankara, Turkey	105	127
Riyadh, Saudi Arabia	106	123
Guadalajara, Mexico	107	116
Abu Dhabi, United Arab Emirates	108	66
Bucharest, Romania	109	110
Curitiba, Brazil	110	129
Bogota, Colombia	111	111
Monterrey, Mexico	112	102
Istanbul, Turkey	113	109
Tunis, Tunisia	114	144
Dubai, United Arab Emirates	115	65

City	Environment Ranking	CIMI 2015 Ranking
Cape Town, South Africa	116	120
Durban, South Africa	117	159
Buenos Aires, Argentina	118	85
Miami, United States	119	53
Lima, Peru	120	122
Santa Cruz, Bolivia	121	171
Skopje, Macedonia	122	146
Phoenix, United States	123	40
Los Angeles, United States	124	15
Alexandria, Egypt	125	173
Casablanca, Morocco	126	163
Philadelphia, United States	127	23
Cali, Colombia	128	126
Sarajevo, Bosnia and Herzegovina	129	157
Guatemala City, Guatemala	130	161
Rio de Janeiro, Brazil	131	139
Moscow, Russia	132	108
Dallas, United States	133	19
Caracas, Venezuela	134	162
La Paz, Bolivia	135	168
Manama, Bahrein	136	138
Salvador, Brazil	137	151
Baku, Azerbaijan	138	150
Sao Paulo, Brazil	139	124
Kiev, Ukraine	140	143
Fortaleza, Brazil	141	149
Amman, Jordan	142	160
Ho Chi Minh City, Vietnam	143	158
Houston, United States	144	31

City	Environment Ranking	CIMI 2015 Ranking
Guayaquil, Ecuador	145	148
Belo Horizonte, Brazil	146	152
Saint Petersburg, Russia	147	133
Doha, Qatar	148	117
Recife, Brazil	149	142
Pretoria, South Africa	150	164
Bangkok, Thailand	151	84
Mexico City, Mexico	152	100
Johannesburg, South Africa	153	140
Novosibirsk, Russia	154	154
Tehran, Iran	155	177
Douala, Cameroon	156	175
Manila, Philippines	157	145
Santo Domingo, Dominican Republic	158	172
Cairo, Egypt	159	156
Jakarta, Indonesia	160	170
Nairobi, Kenya	161	178
Shenzhen, China	162	130
Kaohsiung, Taiwan	163	103
Guangzhou, China	164	104
Bangalore, India	165	176
Lagos, Nigeria	166	180
Taichung, Taiwan	167	112
Taipei, Taiwan	168	64
Karachi, Pakistan	169	181
Bombay, India	170	167
Kolkata, India	171	179
Tainan, Taiwan	172	141

City	Environment Ranking	CIMI 2015 Ranking
Shanghai, China	173	93
Chongqing, China	174	147
Suzhou, China	175	165
Tianjin, China	176	166
Shenyang, China	177	155
Harbin, China	177	169
Wuhan, China	178	153
Beijing, China	179	92
Delhi, India	180	174

Notes